Kingdom Living Everyday

31 Day Devotional Journal

Terri Sparks

Kingdom Reign Publishing
SPREADING THE GOOD NEWS

Kingdom Reign Publishing

Scripture quotations marked (NIV) are taken from
The Holy Bible, New International Version®, NIV®.
Copyright © 1973, 1978, 1984, 2011 by Biblica, Inc.™
Used by permission. All rights reserved worldwide.

Scripture quotations marked (NLT) are taken from
The Holy Bible, New Living Translation,
copyright © 1996, 2004, 2015 by Tyndale House Foundation.
Used by permission of Tyndale House Publishers, Carol Stream, Illinois 60188.
All rights reserved.

Scripture quotations marked (MSG) are taken from *The Message.*
Copyright © 1993, 1994, 1995, 1996, 2000, 2001, 2002 by Eugene H. Peterson.
Used by permission of NavPress. All rights reserved.
Represented by Tyndale House Publishers.

Scripture quotations marked (ESV) are from
The Holy Bible, English Standard Version® (ESV®).
Copyright © 2001 by Crossway, a publishing ministry of Good News Publishers.
Used by permission. All rights reserved.

Scripture quotations marked (GNT) are from
Good News Translation® (Today's English Version, Second Edition).

KINGDOM LIVING EVERYDAY

Author Photo: Terri Sparks

Cover Layout and Manuscript Formatting: Tiffany Tombre

ISBN: 979-8-9926890-6-8

PRINTED IN THE UNITED STATES OF AMERICA

Contents

About the Author
Terri Sparks

Dedication

For every person who refuses to settle for survival and chooses to walk in the fullness of God's promises. May this book remind you that God's plan for you is to live out His will, on earth as it is in Heaven, thriving not just surviving!

Acknowledgements

To my Kingdom Living Everyday family — thank you for being a part of this journey with me. Your faith, encouragement, and hunger for God's truth have inspired every page of this book. You remind me daily what it means to live with kingdom purpose. Your prayers and engagement in this community mean the world to me and you are proof that faith in action changes everything.

To my husband — thank you for believing in me, listening patiently as I sorted through my thoughts and videos, and for helping me bring them into focus. Your love and unwavering support have been an anchor for me. Thank you for always reminding me of God's faithfulness.

To my publisher and editor — Tiffany Tombre and Sarah Simonic, thank you for believing in this message and helping bring it to life with excellence and care. Your guidance, encouragement all along the way, and your great attention to detail refined this book into something I'm truly proud of. I'm deeply grateful for your partnership and for the heart you bring to helping authors share God-inspired words with the world.

And above all, to God — the Author of my life and the source of every word written here. May all glory and honor return to You. And may every person who reads this book know the extent to which You love them and desire for them to walk in the victory You have provided for them.

Introduction

Hi Friends! I think it's time for us to journey together on a challenge! I am confident that if you will dig in with me for the entire month (31 days) and be intentional to focus on HIS promises despite what is happening around you, that you will hear HIM like never before, and you will find yourself walking through your circumstances, your valley, maybe a season, in victory!

Does living in victory every day mean everything will always go your way? We all know that's not the case. But we do know this: The Lord's Prayer says, *"Our Father which art in heaven, hallowed be thy name. Thy kingdom come, thy will be done, on earth as it is in heaven."* Friends, that is God's plan for us. Even in, and especially in, the hard times, HIS way of living and HIS way of doing things (*thy will be done*) is happening in our lives here on earth. Did you hear that? HERE ON EARTH, just as it is in heaven! And, when we learn this and live this way, we can always walk through our trials with confidence that HE is with us, and He will bring us to the other side!

Living in victory every day is a great way to live. So, the assignment for this month is to read a "promise", or a "principle" from the Word of God each day that will help shift your focus ONTO the greatness of our God, and the never-failing, never-ending love He has for us, and to know that He has given us the keys through HIS Word for kingdom living every single day!

This is more of a 31-day FOCUS, instead of CHALLENGE, but I assure you it will also challenge every one of us if we will commit to be intentional to shift our thinking to what God says and thinks about us! So, welcome to 31 days of focusing on God's Words, His principles about you! Each day will contain a solid principle straight from the Bible, with an accompanying key verse for that day. I know that if you apply and incorporate these principles in your life on a daily basis you will find yourself living in victory even when you didn't think it was possible! I don't presume that everything I share will be new news, but my hope and prayer is that what you read and study will send you into deep thinking and application of the Word of God! So, let's get started!

Day 1

I Am Who He Says I Am

PROVERBS 23:7, NKJV - "As a man thinks in his heart, so is he."

Simple, right? YES! It really is! So, why is it that so many believers struggle to see themselves the way God does? You see, I come from a rich heritage of faith. My life from birth has been great. My life, through all the years, through every season, has been great. Truly a firm foundation. But I didn't always have the revelation of "who I was in Christ" that I do now!

In 1998, my husband, Brent & I began attending an annual conference that absolutely CHANGED OUR LIVES! It changed our thinking. It opened our eyes, our minds, our hearts to see ourselves as God sees us. Every year that we would attend, the revelation of WHO WE ARE IN CHRIST became stronger and stronger, and from that beginning, we were able to realize the authority we have in Christ. (We will talk about that another day!)

I don't think you would argue against today's principle, nor do I think you doubt its truth. But, believing it to be true, and walking in the *freedom* that comes from applying the truth of that promise, are two different things. I know many who go through life viewing themselves as a "victim." I don't say that to belittle or knock your pain or struggle, but I can't find anywhere in scripture where you will find God labeling us a victim. Quite the opposite. His Word says, *"I am the head, not the tail."* Deuteronomy 28:13; *"I am above only, not beneath."* Deuteronomy 28:13; *"I can do ALL things through Christ who gives me strength."* Philippians 4:13; *"No weapon formed against me shall prosper."* Isaiah 54:17; *"My steps are ordered of the Lord."* Psalms 37:23; *"He is my Shepherd, I do not want for anything."* Psalms 23:1; *"He is my provider, Jehovah Jireh."* Genesis 22:14; *"My healer, Jehovah Rapha."* Exodus 15:26. So, you see? There's no way we are the victim! *"I am more than a conqueror...an overcomer through Jesus Christ."* Romans 8:37; *"He supplies ALL of my needs."* Philippians 4:19.

In case you didn't know, every single statement that I just quoted is straight out of scripture! So, will you meditate on this today? You ARE who He says you are! When that promise enters your belief system, you will notice a difference. Make no mistake, the devil is going to come at you with lies (that's his job) and try to discredit God's promises to you. Just ignore him and keep shifting your thinking towards God's word! Just one word from God can change your entire life!

How did today's principle impact you?

_____

_____

_____

_____

_____

Is this something you practice consistently, or is there any area that needs improvement?

_____

_____

_____

_____

_____

How can you take today's principle and apply it to your daily routine?

_____

_____

_____

_____

Prayer enlisting the Lord's help to grow in this discipline

_____

_____

_____

_____

List five things you are grateful for in the last 24 hours

1._____

2._____

3._____

4._____

5._____

List five dreams or goals that you are expecting to happen

1._____

2._____

3._____

4._____

5._____

List your top five "daily affirmations" based on the Word, starting with "I Am....."

1._____

2._____

3._____

4._____

5._____

NOTES

_____
_____
_____
_____
_____
_____
_____
_____
_____
_____
_____
_____
_____
_____
_____

Day 2

If the Bible says it I Believe it

I PETER 1:25, NKJV - "But the word of the Lord endures (or remains) forever."

So, this principle—"If the Bible says it, I believe it!"—sounds simple, right? That's because it really *is* that simple. But sometimes I think the problem with people and this principle is they just don't know enough of what the Bible says. Now, I don't say that in a judgmental way, it's just a fact. Hosea 4:6 says, *"My people are destroyed (or perish) for lack of knowledge..."* When we don't know The Word, when we don't have the knowledge that it gives us to live a victorious life, we will eventually be destroyed—we will perish.

That is one reason that if you were to attend or visit our church, we are continually saying, "Read your Bible." It is the Christian's very lifeline. And if we don't know what The Word says, we are going to have a hard time applying it to our lives when the storms come! And they are going to come.

The question is, when the storms come, what do you do? Do you turn to The Word? Do you believe what The Word says about your situation, even when you don't see your situation changing? Or do you get tired and frustrated just "waiting" or "hoping" for change to come? There's a scripture in Ephesians 6 that says, *"...and having done all, to stand."* You're going to have to make the decision to believe what the Bible says. And, when I've done everything I know to do, I will continue to STAND on The Word and believe that God's got me! That HE is in control! And I am resolved to believe His Word.

You absolutely can do this! You just have to make the decision that come what may, you will believe what the Bible says, and nothing, or nobody, can or will take that from you. When you do this, you are on your way to living in victory every day!

How did today's principle impact you?

_____

_____

_____

_____

_____

Is this something you practice consistently, or is there any area that needs improvement?

_____

_____

_____

_____

How can you take today's principle and apply it to your daily routine?

_____

_____

_____

_____

Prayer enlisting the Lord's help to grow in this discipline

_____

_____

_____

_____

_____

List five things you are grateful for in the last 24 hours

1._____

2._____

3._____

4._____

5._____

List five dreams or goals that you are expecting to happen

1._____

2._____

3._____

4._____

5._____

List your top five "daily affirmations" based on the Word, starting with "I Am....."

1._____

2._____

3._____

4._____

5._____

NOTES

Day 3

Get Specific - Find Some Scriptures For Your Specific Need

ISAIAH 55:11, NKJV - "So shall My word be that goes forth from My mouth; It shall not return to Me void (empty), But it shall accomplish what I please, And it shall prosper in the thing for which I sent it."

On days one and two we established the principles that we are who God says we are, and if He said it, I resolve to believe it. Now, if these concepts are new to you, I want to encourage you to make the decision that you're going to give this a shot! I know God will meet you where you are and you will end this month with zero doubts that He has a great plan and purpose for you and that He is the answer you need for everything in life!

Remember yesterday, *"...and having done all, to stand."* I cannot tell you how many situations, circumstances, trials or needs that my family and I have personally walked through over the years; where we have found scriptures to stand on, specific to our current need (whether it was finances, health, wisdom, direction, or peace). You see, life comes along and brings you unexpected news or catches you off guard or is just downright unfair. You're confused, you're sad, you're hurting. I can assure you that you are going to need to get some scriptures that are specific to your current need. Now, let me tell you what to do with those scriptures. Write them down in a journal or on index cards, post them where you can see them, and then say them out loud morning, noon, and night—just like food is nourishment for your body, they are nourishment for your soul.

Just as our scripture for today reads: God's Word is powerful! And His Word does not return to Him empty!

You will NEVER EVER go wrong when you speak God's Word over your situation. Even if the situation doesn't flesh out the way *you* think it should, what I do know is that even if the situation doesn't change, YOU will be changed. I can share that from experience, and I'm telling you, this is how you make it in a cruel world, thriving, not just surviving. Get specific. Go to God's Word and find scriptures for where you are right now. Find some specific scriptures you can stand on.

How did today's principle impact you?

_____

_____

_____

_____

_____

Is this something you practice consistently, or is there any area that needs improvement?

_____

_____

_____

_____

How can you take today's principle and apply it to your daily routine?

_____

_____

_____

_____

Prayer enlisting the Lord's help to grow in this discipline

_____

_____

_____

_____

_____

List five things you are grateful for in the last 24 hours

1._____

2._____

3._____

4._____

5._____

List five dreams or goals that you are expecting to happen

1._____

2._____

3._____

4._____

5._____

List your top five "daily affirmations" based on the Word, starting with "I Am....."

1._____

2._____

3._____

4._____

5._____

NOTES

Day 4

A Firm Foundation is Mandatory (Necessary) for Victory

MATTHEW 7:24-25, NASB - "Therefore everyone who hears these words of Mine and acts on them, may be compared to a wise man who built his house on the rock. And the rain fell, and the floods came, and the winds blew and slammed against that house; and yet it did not fall, for it had been founded on the rock."

I'm glad I get to insert this principle here today! I know the previous three days have been pretty basic...but starting with the basics is super important to creating a foundation! When you apply these principles that we've already talked about, you are doing just that! And it's a really great place to start!

Here's what the Bible says about foundations. First, let's read our key verse for today, and add a few more to it. Matthew 7:24-27 (NASB), *"Therefore everyone who hears these words of Mine and acts on them, may be compared to a wise man who built his house on the rock. And the rain fell, and the floods came, and the winds blew and slammed against that house; and yet it did not fall, for it had been founded on the rock. And everyone who hears these words of Mine, and does not act on them, will be like a foolish man who built his house on the sand. And the rain fell and the floods came, and the winds blew and slammed against that house; and it fell—and its collapse was great."*

This passage actually comes at the end of Jesus's well-known "Sermon on the Mount". As He taught the people on that mountain, He gave them a lot of instructions on how to live—what TO do and what NOT to do. In closing His sermon, He defines two groups of people: those who hear His words and act on them, and those who hear His words but do not act on them. Their obedience to His teaching determines who is compared to a wise man, and who is compared to a foolish man, and the results that accompany each one of them. A house built on the rock, or a house built on the sand—one stands through it all, the other has a great collapse!

If it was important enough for Jesus to teach these principles and instructions in depth to the people—I mean, like three whole chapters' worth!—then it's important enough for us to read our Bible and know what it says (which is the equivalent of His teaching and us hearing), so that we are ones who both "hear" and "act". Basically: read The Word, and then do what it says! Then, we will be like the wise man who built his house on the rock—we will have a firm foundation! And that is mandatory—necessary—for living in victory every single day.

How did today's principle impact you?

_____

_____

_____

_____

_____

Is this something you practice consistently, or is there any area that needs improvement?

_____

_____

_____

_____

How can you take today's principle and apply it to your daily routine?

_____

_____

_____

_____

Prayer enlisting the Lord's help to grow in this discipline

_____

_____

_____

_____

List five things you are grateful for in the last 24 hours

1._____
2._____
3._____
4._____
5._____

List five dreams or goals that you are expecting to happen

1._____
2._____
3._____
4._____
5._____

List your top five "daily affirmations" based on the Word, starting with "I Am....."

1._____
2._____
3._____
4._____
5._____

NOTES

NOTES

Day 5

Live Each Day - One Day at a Time and Don't Worry About Tomorrow

MATTHEW 6:25, THE VOICE - "Here is the bottom line: do not worry about your life."

Matthew 6:27, The Voice - "Worrying does not do any good; who here can claim to add even an hour to his life by worrying?"

Matthew 6:34, The Voice - "So do not worry about tomorrow. Let tomorrow worry about itself. Living faithfully is a large enough task for today."

Well, after yesterday's talk about Jesus' "Sermon on the Mount," I was curious as to what other instructions and principles He gave us through that sermon. So, listen to what Matthew 6 in The Voice Translation says.

Vs. 25-26: *"Here is the bottom line: do not worry about your life. Look at the birds in the sky. They do not store food for winter. They don't plant gardens.*

They do not sow or reap—and yet, they are always fed because your heavenly Father feeds them. And you are even more precious to Him than a beautiful bird. If He looks after them, of course He will look after you."

Vs. 27-29: *"Worrying does not do any good; who here can claim to add even an hour to his life by worrying? Consider the lilies of the field and how they grow. They do not work or weave or sew, and yet their garments are stunning. Even King Solomon, dressed in his most regal garb, was not as lovely as these lilies."* Vs. 33-34: *"Seek first the kingdom of God and His righteousness, and then all these things will be given to you too. So do not worry about tomorrow. Let tomorrow worry about itself. Living faithfully is a large enough task for today."*

Jesus says worrying does not do any good, and when we seek God and His Kingdom first, HE WILL provide all we need. He compares our worries about lacking provision to the provisions given to the birds and flowers. He says, *"Look at the birds! If He looks after them, of course He will look after you! Consider the lilies of the field! Even King Solomon in his most regal garb was not as lovely as these lilies!"*

And, instead of worrying, we are to SEEK FIRST the KINGDOM of GOD and His Righteousness, and then ALL THESE THINGS will be given to us! You see? When we do things God's way, when we seek Him first and make Him our priority, we don't have to live a life of worry! We are confident that He will provide what we need! Then He closes out chapter six by saying, in verse 34, *"So do not worry about tomorrow! Let tomorrow worry about itself."* Our job is to seek God first, and focus on living faithfully each day, one day at a time!

How did today's principle impact you?

_____

_____

_____

_____

_____

Is this something you practice consistently, or is there any area that needs improvement?

_____

_____

_____

_____

How can you take today's principle and apply it to your daily routine?

_____

_____

_____

_____

Prayer enlisting the Lord's help to grow in this discipline

_____

_____

_____

_____

_____

List five things you are grateful for in the last 24 hours

1._____

2._____

3._____

4._____

5._____

List five dreams or goals that you are expecting to happen

1._____

2._____

3._____

4._____

5._____

List your top five "daily affirmations" based on the Word, starting with "I Am....."

1._____

2._____

3._____

4._____

5._____

NOTES

NOTES

Day 6

Walk By Faith Not By Sight

2 CORINTHIANS 5:7, NKJV - "For we walk by faith, not by sight."

Yesterday we talked about how we should live each day, one day at a time, and not to worry. But we all know that in life we are going to have things come at us that are unexpected, and quite frankly, unwelcomed! So how do we navigate the "living, and not worrying" principle? I'm glad you asked! Because THIS is why we are doing what we are doing in this devotional. We are learning how to build a foundation, so that when something blindsides you and leaves you in tears (which is a normal reaction), that you are able to get the tears out—that initial cry. And while there may be more (you're not inhuman), in the middle of it all you reach down deep and you say, "Okay, I know who God says I am; I know what the Word says, and I believe it; and I'm going to find some scriptures that speak to this—that's my foundation!"

God tells us, "Don't worry about tomorrow." So, let's figure out what we have to do to make it through faithfully and not worry about today or tomorrow. This process and order of "To Do's" is how you navigate the unexpected, unwelcomed things that life throws at you. If you are able to do this, you will find yourself calmer than you thought you might be—surprisingly calm! You know why? Because you are walking by faith! We are called as believers to *"Walk by faith, not by sight."* If we go by only what we see, then we may be tempted to crumble underneath the weight and the overwhelming burden that life, THIS life, brings us.

So as believers, we're going to stand upon our firm foundation; we're going to do all the things we know to do. We are going to pray (we haven't even touched on this great principle yet, but we KNOW to do that!), put on worship music and praise the Lord, get scriptures that are specific to your needs, get the Word out! Look at our scripture for today's principle: *"For we walk by faith, not by sight."* Some translations say, *"We live by faith, not by sight."* Another translation says, *"It is by believing that we live, not by seeing."* Aren't you thankful for our faith in God and in His Word—His promises to us as believers—that when we are doing OUR part, He is going to come through and do HIS part? Now, it may not be in our timing! We might muddle through a few days in tears and in "commanding our soul" (like the song "Gratitude"); we COMMAND our soul to praise the Lord, even in the valley! That's what it does—it presses us to go on. We walk by faith, not by sight, and that's the trust we have!

Even when we don't see it, we know He's working and it's going to work out! So, friend, before you get slammed with life, do all that you can to make sure your foundation is firmly built, then trust that your house is not going to fall when the storms rage! It may weather the storm, which is not pleasant, and not always easy, but that's what walking by faith is, and that's what we are called to do. Be encouraged today. Walk by faith, not by sight. It's faith that keeps us believing, even when we don't see it.

How did today's principle impact you?

_____

_____

_____

_____

_____

Is this something you practice consistently, or is there any area that needs improvement?

_____

_____

_____

_____

How can you take today's principle and apply it to your daily routine?

_____

_____

_____

_____

_____

Prayer enlisting the Lord's help to grow in this discipline

_____

_____

_____

_____

List five things you are grateful for in the last 24 hours

1._____
2._____
3._____
4._____
5._____

List five dreams or goals that you are expecting to happen

1._____
2._____
3._____
4._____
5._____

List your top five "daily affirmations" based on the Word, starting with "I Am....."

1._____
2._____
3._____
4._____
5._____

NOTES

_____
_____
_____
_____
_____
_____
_____
_____
_____
_____
_____
_____
_____
_____
_____

Day 7

God is a Supernatural Being - Therefore He Operates in the Supernatural

ISAIAH 55:8-9, NLT: "'MY thoughts are nothing like your thoughts,' says the Lord. 'And my ways are far beyond anything you could imagine. For just as the heavens are higher than the earth, so my ways are higher than your ways and my thoughts higher than your thoughts.'"

Day seven. The principle today is, "God is a supernatural being, therefore He operates in the supernatural." What that means for us as believers is that HIS WAYS are not always our ways. We don't even think like Him most of the time! But what we must do is put all these principles that we've been reading about into place so that we have a firm foundation. We just believe what the Word says. We believe we are who He says we are. And we're walking by faith and not by sight.

We have to understand that the ways we **hope** that God will move, or that **we believe** God will come through in our specific need, may not be the way He sees best for us. And you know what? It might just be because we are short-changing Him. We might be asking Him to do something that's really small and He's thinking, "That's just too small, I've got a better plan for you. My plan is going to blow your mind! It's supernatural!" And when you think you're at a dead end, God is saying, "I need you to sit back and walk by faith and just trust me. You've got your foundation built, and I need you to not look at what it looks like in the natural, but I need you to know that I'm working in the SUPERnatural realm." According to dictionary.com, the word supernatural means: **of, relating to, or being above or beyond what is natural; unexplainable by natural law or phenomena; abnormal.**

And that is the kind of God we serve. I was thinking of a couple of instances in the Word where supernatural things happened. And believe it or not, these are all in the Bible and you can easily read them for yourself. In the book of Numbers, I see where Balaam, who was a magician of sorts, a diviner, told the future. He had a donkey that spoke to him. And I think that is the wildest thing that I could imagine—if the donkey you're riding on would just stop and turn around and speak, that's crazy! It's supernatural! But God needed to get a message through to Balaam. He used the donkey to talk because Balaam was not paying attention to Him. Have you ever been guilty of that? Not paying attention to what God's trying to say to you? I have.

Or look at Daniel! Remember the Bible story from your childhood? Maybe some of you do. He vowed to not bow to anyone other than His God, the one true God, even though a serious decree had gone out in the kingdom with severe punishment—a trip to the lion's den—for anyone who refused to bow to the King. Hungry, hungry lions who had not been fed.

Still Daniel did not bow. So when the King's officials threw Daniel into the lion's den, they thought he would be eaten up in no time. Those lions did not even go near him. That's supernatural! What about the three Hebrew youth, Shadrach, Meshach, and Abednego who were thrown into a fire? A fire so hot that it burned and killed the guards who threw them in! But that's not all! Jesus ended up showing up in the fire. All four men walked around in the fire, like "no big deal," then the three Hebrew guys walked right out of the fire, not even smelling like smoke. Friends, that's supernatural!

So while you're just praying for something over here, God's thinking, if you'll just sit back and let me work, you'll see what I'm going to do! Now, I'm not saying don't pray. By all means, pray. But you might have pigeonholed a certain answer you're looking for because God's up there thinking, "I'm going to do so much more than that in a much crazier way than you could ever imagine!" And you just have to say, okay, I give it to you, God, I lay it at your feet! You know better than I do.

The Bible says that His ways are higher than my ways and that His thoughts are higher than my thoughts. They're not my thoughts. They're better! That's what you'll find in Isaiah 55:8-9, and that's where our principle comes from today. He's a supernatural God and He is here to meet your needs. Even when it looks impossible. We still have to do our part. That's why we're going through this month to remind ourselves to establish a FIRM FOUNDATION. This is what we must do to position ourselves. It's then that we can sit back and do what we're supposed to do—look for

an impossible situation to be answered by a supernatural God. He's just
that good.

How did today's principle impact you?

_____

_____

_____

_____

_____

Is this something you practice consistently, or is there any area that needs improvement?

_____

_____

_____

_____

How can you take today's principle and apply it to your daily routine?

_____

_____

_____

_____

Prayer enlisting the Lord's help to grow in this discipline

_____

_____

_____

_____

_____

List five things you are grateful for in the last 24 hours

1._____

2._____

3._____

4._____

5._____

List five dreams or goals that you are expecting to happen

1._____

2._____

3._____

4._____

5._____

List your top five "daily affirmations" based on the Word, starting with "I Am....."

1._____

2._____

3._____

4._____

5._____

NOTES

NOTES

Day 8

Wholeheartedly

NUMBERS 32:11, NLT: *"OF ALL THOSE I rescued from Egypt, no one who is twenty years old or older will ever see the land I swore to give to Abraham, Isaac, and Jacob, <u>for they have not obeyed me wholeheartedly.</u>"*

Today's principle is one word. Wholeheartedly. That just speaks for itself. Wholeheartedly simply means, **with your whole heart**. This ties in nicely with the previous principles we've covered. As I was reading my Bible plan this morning something jumped off the page at me and got me thinking. Do you know one of the reasons, one of the main reasons, the children of Israel did not get to cross over into the Promised Land? Let's look at our key verse from Numbers 32:11 once again: *"Of all those I rescued from Egypt, no one who is twenty years old or older will ever see the land I swore to give to Abraham, Isaac, and Jacob, <u>for they have not obeyed me wholeheartedly.</u>"*

Man, what a terrible shame! They will never see the land—that's what God said. Not only will they not get to go into the promised land, but they will never even SEE the land that He swore to give to Abraham, Isaac, and Jacob. All because they did not obey Him wholeheartedly. And then the next verse says that the ONLY exceptions are Caleb and Joshua. For God said they **wholeheartedly** followed the Lord. My challenge to you today is to take a look at where you are on your journey right now, the needs you're facing, the mountains in front of you, and in light of what you see, can you say that you are wholeheartedly following the Lord? Are you obeying Him with your whole heart?

I thought of this story in the New Testament from Mark chapter nine, of the demon possessed boy. The father brought him to Jesus and pleaded with Jesus asking Him to help them. But his way of asking was more like, *"Help us, if you can!" And Jesus answers, "What do you mean if I can?"* He then tells the boy's father that anything is possible, IF you believe. And immediately the father answered, *"Oh, Jesus, yes, I do believe,"*—but then he followed it up with, *"But help me with my unbelief."* You might be thinking, "How can that be? Surely that can't be true." But I say yes, it is true. And unfortunately, a lot of believers find themselves in this very same scenario. They have belief AND unbelief at the same time. I remember years ago I was traveling to Houston to see a friend who was sick in the hospital, and things in the natural realm did not look good. And I remember praying to the Lord, *"God, I know you can heal him, but I just don't know if you will."* Both belief and unbelief. And I think that's where we sometimes find ourselves. We know God can. We don't really have a problem believing what the Word says or believing that God CAN do what He says He can do. The breakdown comes like this: I know He CAN, I just don't know if He WILL.

I hope this principle today will push you (in a good way) to grow in your thinking so that you can mature in your believing and grow your faith. You know—that level to which you can look at the natural and still see with your spiritual eyes that if God said it, I wholeheartedly believe not just that He CAN do it, but that He WILL do it. And just settle in your spirit that you're not going to take anything less. God said it. I believe it, and that's with my WHOLE heart. No unbelief here. I will believe what He says about me, and I'm going to walk this life in victory because He said, *"Anything is possible to him who believes."*

So, check your heart today and decide that from this day forward, "I'm going to believe with my whole heart. I'm going to follow Him with my whole heart. I'm going to obey Him with my whole heart. Wholeheartedly."

How did today's principle impact you?

_____

_____

_____

_____

Is this something you practice consistently, or is there any area that needs improvement?

_____

_____

_____

How can you take today's principle and apply it to your daily routine?

_____

_____

_____

_____

_____

Prayer enlisting the Lord's help to grow in this discipline

_____

_____

_____

_____

List five things you are grateful for in the last 24 hours

1._____
2._____
3._____
4._____
5._____

List five dreams or goals that you are expecting to happen

1._____
2._____
3._____
4._____
5._____

List your top five "daily affirmations" based on the Word, starting with "I Am....."

1._____
2._____
3._____
4._____
5._____

NOTES

Day 9

Be Still and Know that He is God

PSALMS 46:10, NIV: "...BE still, and know that I am God..."

There are a lot of people dealing with a lot of stuff right now and I pray you are encouraged today as we talk about this principle, this scripture, to "Be still and know that He is God." While this verse does encourage us to focus on who God is and to simply rest in Him, it's actually more of a wake-up call for believers to stop fearing and acknowledge who God is—to be in awe of Him! Let me read this verse in a few other translations:

"Be still, be calm, see, and understand I am the True God." The Voice

"Step out of the traffic! Take a long, loving look at me, your High God, above everything." The MSG

This goes hand in hand with the fact that God is supernatural, and we have to keep our eyes on HIM and believe HIS WORD over what we see in the natural! He's above, beyond, far higher and far greater!

So, looking at Psalm 46, this entire chapter was written during a time of trouble and war, but look how the chapter begins. *"God is our refuge and strength, a very present help in trouble. Therefore we will not fear..."* and the writers, a group of temple musicians and Levites called the Sons of Korah, lists examples of things to not fear. Then the chapter ends reminding us to *"Be still and know..."* or to "Stop! Remember WHO YOU SERVE!" *"...The Commander of heavenly armies..."*

Here I am, over here thinking the "be still" part simply meant to rest. And, it does! BUT now I'm also looking at it as, "Stop fighting, stop trying to control things in your own strength, and focus on GOD and be in AWE of HIM!" I want to close today by quoting from an article I read online at crosswalk.com, entitled "What Does 'Be Still and Know that I am God' Really Mean". I believe someone needs to hear it today!

"His Word reminds us who He is and calls us to worship in awe. Be still and remember who God is, be still and stop fearing, be still and see what God is doing, be still and acknowledge His greatness, be still and know God is with you..."

Be still and know that He is God.

How did today's principle impact you?

_____

_____

_____

_____

_____

Is this something you practice consistently, or is there any area that needs improvement?

_____

_____

_____

_____

How can you take today's principle and apply it to your daily routine?

_____

_____

_____

_____

Prayer enlisting the Lord's help to grow in this discipline

_____

_____

_____

_____

List five things you are grateful for in the last 24 hours

1._____
2._____
3._____
4._____
5._____

List five dreams or goals that you are expecting to happen

1._____
2._____
3._____
4._____
5._____

List your top five "daily affirmations" based on the Word, starting with "I Am....."

1._____
2._____
3._____
4._____
5._____

NOTES

Day 10

Trust God in the Waiting - He is Always Working

JOHN 5:17, NLT - *"But Jesus replied, 'My Father is always working, and so am I.'"*

Today we see again, the promise that He is always working is found in scripture. Clearly, John 5:17 tells us so. But let's also look at a few other scriptures. Philippians 2:13 says, *"For it is God who is at work in you, both to will and to work for His good pleasure."*

Isaiah 45:15 in The Message says, *"Clearly, you are a God who works behind the scenes,"* OR another translation reads, *"You work in mysterious ways."*

Mysterious ways. We know that His ways are higher than our ways, and His thoughts are higher than our thoughts. And sometimes we don't even recognize that He is working! But He has a bird's eye view, and He sees the big picture, when we can only see in part. We only see the part that's right in front of us, the natural part. That's when you have to resolve to trust God, especially in the waiting!

There is a song titled "Waymaker" that says, "Even when I don't see it, You're working; Even when I don't feel it, You're working! You never stop, You never stop working! You never stop, You never stop working!" God knows what we need, what is best for us. And He never takes a day off, not even a minute off! So, while He is working, how do you trust God in the waiting?

Psalm 37:7, ESV says, *"Be still in the presence of the Lord, and wait patiently for him to act."* What I want you to grasp here is how to position yourself to wait. **In His Presence!** While you are waiting (patiently, that is), stay in His presence. How? In prayer. Talk to God and then listen for Him to respond to you. Read your Bible for this is a major way He speaks to you. The Bible is His words on paper. Listen to worship music. These are super practical ways to discover and experience God's presence, and they are equally super important. You see, He will be where you welcome Him to be! Right there with you. And in His presence is where you will find everything you need to get you through what you're going through, while you wait.

Here's an encouraging verse I want to leave with you to meditate on today:

Isaiah 40:31, ESV - *"But they who wait for (trust in) the Lord shall renew their strength; they shall mount up with wings like eagles; they shall run and not be weary; they shall walk and not faint."*

Trust God in the waiting. Sit still in His presence. Be patient. He is always working.

How did today's principle impact you?

_____

_____

_____

_____

Is this something you practice consistently, or is there any area that needs improvement?

_____

_____

_____

_____

How can you take today's principle and apply it to your daily routine?

_____

_____

_____

_____

Prayer enlisting the Lord's help to grow in this discipline

_____

_____

_____

_____

List five things you are grateful for in the last 24 hours

1._____

2._____

3._____

4._____

5._____

List five dreams or goals that you are expecting to happen

1._____

2._____

3._____

4._____

5._____

List your top five "daily affirmations" based on the Word, starting with "I Am....."

1._____

2._____

3._____

4._____

5._____

List five things you are grateful for in the last 24 hours

1.

2.

3.

4.

5.

List five dreams or goals that I want to see that I pray appear

1.

2.

3.

4.

5.

List your top five faith affirmations based on the word starting with "I am"

1.

2.

3.

4.

5.

NOTES

_____
_____
_____
_____
_____
_____
_____
_____
_____
_____
_____
_____
_____
_____
_____

NOTES

Day 11

Be Willing and Obedient

ISAIAH 1:19-20, ESV - *"If you are willing and obedient, you shall eat the good of the land; but if you refuse and rebel, you shall be eaten by the sword; for the mouth of the Lord has spoken."*

Okay, as we begin today's reading, let's read our scripture again in another translation. The Voice Translation reads this way, *"If you pay attention now and change your ways, you can eat good things from a healthy earth. But if you refuse to listen and stubbornly persist, then, by violence and war, you will be the one devoured."*

Here in Isaiah 1, God has urged the people of Israel to stop their meaningless worship rituals and to change the way they are living. He is still upset with them for their rebellion and wickedness, and He is still giving them instructions on how to live His way! We also still see His deep love for His people, and if they are willing to obey Him, He will wipe away their wrongdoings and make them clean and pour out blessings on them!

I love this next part, so I want to read it from the bibleref.com commentary:

Though the Lord is clear in His instructions, this will require the Israelites to be intentional about how they live. They must be wholehearted participants in pursuing to obey Him. If they do so, He will bring prosperity to them. He will give them all they need, including safety and security from their enemies. The opposite choice will bring starkly different consequences.

It sounds like these instructions are good for us today too, in our everyday life! And did you notice the line that said they must be "wholehearted participants"? Just what we talked about yesterday! WE are God's chosen people! He loves us SO much, even with our shortcomings and failures, and He is willing to wipe away our wrongdoings and make us clean again. And after all that, He will then proceed to pour out blessings on us! And all He really wants from us is to be intentional about how we live and to wholeheartedly obey Him. IF WE DO THIS, He will bring prosperity to us. Prosperity = nothing missing, nothing broken! He will give us ALL WE NEED (safety, security). Then He warns us if we DON'T choose obedience, there will be different consequences. And those consequences are on us, not God, for disobeying Him. He's pretty clear what our path to victory and good living is—so be willing and obedient!

I pray today that you will be intentional in being willing and obedient to Him in every way! It's a pretty important key to living in victory EVERY DAY!

How did today's principle impact you?

_____

_____

_____

_____

_____

Is this something you practice consistently, or is there any area that needs improvement?

_____

_____

_____

_____

How can you take today's principle and apply it to your daily routine?

_____

_____

_____

_____

Prayer enlisting the Lord's help to grow in this discipline

_____

_____

_____

_____

List five things you are grateful for in the last 24 hours

1._____

2._____

3._____

4._____

5._____

List five dreams or goals that you are expecting to happen

1._____

2._____

3._____

4._____

5._____

List your top five "daily affirmations" based on the Word, starting with "I Am....."

1._____

2._____

3._____

4._____

5._____

NOTES

Day 12

Do Not Give Up - Don't Quit - Keep Standing

GALATIANS 6:9, GNT - "So let us not become tired of doing good; for if we do not give up, the time will come when we will reap the harvest."

At the time of this writing, it is a beautiful morning. The birds are singing; my puppies are living their best life outside in the crisp air; and I'm here to give you today's principle, which is, **do not give up. Don't quit. Keep standing.** This principle comes from today's scripture verse, Galatians 6:9 - *"So let us not become tired of doing good; for if we do not give up, the time will come when we will reap the harvest."* So many times we stop too early and give up right before our harvest comes. Some people will get so very, very close. I mean, it's like the next day might be their breakthrough. The next day might be their answered prayer, and they just get tired, and they quit. Let this encourage you to hold on and keep standing.

"*...And having done all, to stand.*" That's what Ephesians 6:13 says we are to do. You just stand and you keep standing—on His Word! People might think, "Well, nothing's happening. God isn't coming through on His end. He must be mad at me." Or "He doesn't hear me. He's not listening. This just isn't going to work." And honestly, it might *appear* that it's not working. And I understand it's easy to get frustrated and distracted. But you can't afford to stop! You can't afford to give up! **Do not give up**. You may feel like you are out there on the brink of quitting and saying, "I am done!" But you know what? You've got to just keep standing.

This principle must become a way of life for you that you learn to live every single day, not just incorporate for a month or two while you're going through a problem. **This is a lifestyle.** This is your new way of thinking, of living, of getting through every single problem that comes your way! It's to help you get a *new* perspective on how you're going to live this lifestyle from here on out, day in and day out, whether you're on the mountain, or in the valley. You're going to decide, "I'm never going to give up!"

I'm never going to get tired of standing and doing what God says to do, because if I press on and hold fast to the Word of God, and *His way of doing things,* I will make it through whatever comes my way. "*Weeping endures for a season, but joy comes in the morning,*" is another great promise from God's Word found in Psalm 30:5. You've got this. You can do this. Surround yourself with other believers who can stand strong with you, who can lift your arms up just like Aaron and Hur did for Moses when they were in battle, as read in Exodus chapter 17. As long as Moses' arms were up, the Israelites were winning. When he got tired and he couldn't do it anymore, and he put his arms down, then the Israelites began to lose their battle. And the people around him recognized that, so they came and picked his arms up and they held them up. They were in it with him. And when his arms were raised—when he was looking up to the Lord and surrendering to Him—the Israelites were victorious, and they ended up winning the battle. You can do this. Find some people—maybe at your church, in your small group, in your household. Find people that will walk with you through the hard times.

Isaiah 40:31 that tells us to *"Wait on the Lord."* Because when you wait on the Lord, you find new strength. You'll find the strength to begin walking, and pretty soon you'll be running. You're going to soar with the eagles. You're not going to get weary. You're not going to faint. There's an old hymn entitled *"Teach Me, Lord, to Wait"*, and that is exactly what we should be praying! So keep standing, keep waiting, keep holding on. You're going to press through to victory, and He's going to carry you through this valley. Then you'll find yourself on top of the mountain helping someone else do the same.

Do not give up.

How did today's principle impact you?

_____

_____

_____

_____

Is this something you practice consistently, or is there any area that needs improvement?

_____

_____

_____

_____

How can you take today's principle and apply it to your daily routine?

_____

_____

_____

_____

Prayer enlisting the Lord's help to grow in this discipline

_____

_____

_____

_____

List five things you are grateful for in the last 24 hours

1._____

2._____

3._____

4._____

5._____

List five dreams or goals that you are expecting to happen

1._____

2._____

3._____

4._____

5._____

List your top five "daily affirmations" based on the Word, starting with "I Am....."

1._____

2._____

3._____

4._____

5._____

List five things you are grateful for in the current hour.

_____

_____

_____

_____

_____

List five thoughts or words that are encouraging to happen

_____

_____

_____

_____

List your top five daily affirmations based on the Word, starting with "I Am."

_____

_____

_____

_____

_____

NOTES

Day 13

We Will Face Hard Times - We Will Get Through Them

John 16:33, NLT - "*I have told you all this so that you may have peace in me. Here on earth you will have many trials and sorrows. But take heart, because I have overcome the world.*"

Again, read this verse with me in The Voice Translation: "*I have told you these things so that you will be whole and at peace. In this world, you will be plagued with times of trouble, but you need not fear; I have triumphed over this corrupt world order.*"

If you look at people around you, you may sense heaviness in many believers and in our family units. People are walking through hard stuff—trials, sorrows, times of trouble. Life happens. Life isn't always fair. Bad things happen to good people. It stinks, really. But, as Christ-followers, we don't stop doing what we know to do, because He told us hard times—challenges—were going to happen.

But just as quickly as He shed light on the fact that troubles would come, He told us how we would get through them in victory. The answer? Peace in Him! PEACE! It IS possible to have peace even when the world around you tells you differently, or the people around you cannot understand how you can walk in peace. It's only through HIM! In John 16:33, NLT, Jesus says, *"I have told you all this so that you may have peace in ME...But take heart!"* And in The Voice Translation notes for John 16 on biblegateway. com, we find where He disarms fear by saying, "If the Spirit is within, there is no reason to fear." Then He says, "Take heart."'

According to Merriam-Webster, "take heart" means to gain courage or confidence; to begin to feel better and more hopeful. Take heart—things will get better soon. Jesus is telling us we can be more hopeful, that these troubles will pass and things will get better soon.

Many of you are facing hard times. It's not fair, it's not fun, and it hurts. It's hard. I want to encourage you today to run TO God, cling TO HIM. HE is the one who will never leave us nor forsake us. I often ponder the questions, "What would I do if I did not have hope? What do non-believers do without the hope that only God can give us?" He cares about you, friend, and He will carry you through to the other side, even if—and when—our prayers don't get answered the way we are asking. We just cling to, or "hold on tightly" to God. He is always with us. Take heart, find peace in Him, and keep standing.

How did today's principle impact you?

_____

_____

_____

_____

_____

Is this something you practice consistently, or is there any area that needs improvement?

_____

_____

_____

_____

How can you take today's principle and apply it to your daily routine?

_____

_____

_____

_____

Prayer enlisting the Lord's help to grow in this discipline

_____

_____

_____

_____

List five things you are grateful for in the last 24 hours

1._____

2._____

3._____

4._____

5._____

List five dreams or goals that you are expecting to happen

1._____

2._____

3._____

4._____

5._____

List your top five "daily affirmations" based on the Word, starting with "I Am....."

1._____

2._____

3._____

4._____

5._____

NOTES

Day 14

The Choice is Ours - WE Get to Choose

DEUTERONOMY 30:19, NLT - "Today I have given you the choice between life and death, between blessings and curses. Now I call on heaven and earth to witness the choice you make. Oh, that you would choose life, so that you and your descendants might live!"

What's happening here in Deuteronomy 30?

After wandering through the desert for 40 years and following God through Moses' leadership, the Israelites were finally ready to enter the Promised Land. But before they did, God needed to get their entire focus and remind them of His authority and the importance of obeying His commands.

He laid out the choices and the consequences of both obedience and disobedience. Isn't that where we find ourselves today? There are choices, and there are consequences. The beauty of it all is that God allows US to choose, but all the while, wholeheartedly wanting us to choose LIFE. Can't you just feel His heart when you read *"Oh that you would choose life so that you and your descendants might live!"*?

I know there are many things in life that happen to us that we don't choose and that we can't control. But what we can control is the choice we make in how we walk through the difficult times. And again, I think back to just yesterday's devotional: how do people who don't have a relationship with God make it through tough times? Where do they put their hope? Do they even have hope?

I'm so thankful for a loving God, who is a good Father, who allows me the ability to choose, but lays it all out for me, showing me the benefits of making the right choice. And that right choice, my friends, is to choose HIS way to live—not mine. He's even so good to tell us how to do this—how to live in victory through it all! Look at the next verse, Deuteronomy 30:20.

Verse 20 - *"You can make this choice by loving the Lord your God, obeying him, and committing yourself firmly to Him. This is the key to your life."*

We just recently studied "be willing and obedient" to His way of life, and the benefits it brings. He's repeating it again here, in a different way, because He so wants us to experience life His way, and to live life in abundance.

So that's my challenge to you today: love the Lord your God, obey Him, and commit firmly to Him. (That's what I hope you see how to do throughout this month's devotions.) Deuteronomy 30:20 ends by saying, *"THIS IS THE KEY TO YOUR LIFE!"*

The choice is ours. WE get to choose.

How did today's principle impact you?

_____

_____

_____

_____

Is this something you practice consistently, or is there any area that needs improvement?

_____

_____

_____

_____

How can you take today's principle and apply it to your daily routine?

_____

_____

_____

_____

Prayer enlisting the Lord's help to grow in this discipline

_____

_____

_____

_____

List five things you are grateful for in the last 24 hours

1._____

2._____

3._____

4._____

5._____

List five dreams or goals that you are expecting to happen

1._____

2._____

3._____

4._____

5._____

List your top five "daily affirmations" based on the Word, starting with "I Am....."

1._____

2._____

3._____

4._____

5._____

List five things you are grateful for in the last 24 hours.

List five dreams or goals that you are expecting to happen.

List your top five "daily affirmations" based on the Word starting with "I Am..."

NOTES

Day 15

Fully Persuaded

ROMANS 4:20-21, NIV - "Yet he did not waver through unbelief regarding the promise of God, but was strengthened in his faith and gave glory to God, being fully persuaded that God had power to do what he had promised."

To be persuaded is to be convinced and to know without doubt. How does this apply to you spiritually, and how can you be fully persuaded?

So, this may seem simple to you, but being fully persuaded comes by consistent, daily exposure to the spoken Word of God. You see, this leads us to speaking out what we believe, or confessing it, which is an act of faith that in turn brings belief. There is great power in our words, and in our confessing of THE Word! Interesting enough is the fact that our brain and our mind play a HUGE role in this process of when we speak out loud and the results we see. Especially when we speak OUT LOUD the Word of God!

There's just something supernatural that happens when you speak The WORD out loud. It may begin as something you just recite, but it will eventually move from recitation to "fully persuaded!" Why don't you find some scriptures that speak to whatever situation you are facing right now, and practice speaking your scriptures over your situation, out loud. Write your scriptures on index cards and carry them with you throughout your day. Then look at them often and read them aloud! There's power in the spoken Word of God, and you are soon on your way to being FULLY PERSUADED. (Again, the results you will see will be tied to the strong connection between what you say and how your brain and mind process that information!)

Let's look at Abraham real quick. He was told he would be the "father of many nations" long before he ever even had a son. And then, after that, he and his wife Sarah waited 25 years for the promised son Isaac to come. 25 long years! But they waited.

The Bible says (talking about Abraham), *"He staggered not at the promise of God through unbelief, but was strong in faith, giving glory to God, and being fully persuaded that what He had promised, He was able also to perform."* That, again, is today's scripture, Romans 4:20–21.

So, here we are, over here just working on getting any and all unbelief OUT of our hearts and minds, and training our mouths to speak what God says, so our brain/mind is renewed and we can walk FULLY PERSUADED! Fully persuaded that what God has promised us, He is able to perform it! This is a great segway into our principles coming for the next few days! So, make today a good day, be fully persuaded, and show up for tomorrow's devotional. We're doing this!

How did today's principle impact you?

_____

_____

_____

_____

_____

Is this something you practice consistently, or is there any area that needs improvement?

_____

_____

_____

_____

How can you take today's principle and apply it to your daily routine?

_____

_____

_____

_____

Prayer enlisting the Lord's help to grow in this discipline

_____

_____

_____

_____

_____

List five things you are grateful for in the last 24 hours

1._____

2._____

3._____

4._____

5._____

List five dreams or goals that you are expecting to happen

1._____

2._____

3._____

4._____

5._____

List your top five "daily affirmations" based on the Word, starting with "I Am....."

1._____

2._____

3._____

4._____

5._____

NOTES

Day 16

Speak to Your Mountain

Mark 11:22-23 The Passion Translation (TPT) - "Jesus replied, 'Let the faith of God be in you! Listen to the truth I speak to you: Whoever says to this mountain with great faith and does not doubt, 'Mountain, be lifted up and thrown into the midst of the sea,' and believes that what he says will happen, it will be done."

Following yesterday's devotional on training our mouths to speak God's Word, here we go. Why is "Speak to your Mountain" an important principle for us believers?

He (Jesus) was preparing us for those times when we would have to take direct authority in the spiritual realm to impact things in the natural realm. There are two main factors to remember here: His authority (the faith of God) and the Spoken Word. Remember yesterday? Fully Persuaded = consistent daily exposure to the Spoken WORD!

Jesus is teaching us a few things here in this passage:

1. That when we come up against a mountain, or a problem, we are to speak TO it, not about it. But here's what happens many times: People end up talking ABOUT their mountains instead of talking TO their mountains. And the more we speak about our problem, the bigger it gets and the more power it has over us and our lives. What you magnify, multiplies. Don't let that be you! Speak TO your mountain.

2. There's certainly nothing wrong with us praying TO God about our "mountains" or our problems. But you need to know that He has given YOU the authority to speak to your mountain yourself. So, get bold, rise up and tell the devil you've had enough of him, enough of this...and then YOU command your mountain to move! This is why it's so very important that you know what the Bible says about your problems! You are going to need some scriptures to speak out loud to your mountain! That's what you're going to "fight" with—God's WORD spoken by YOU! It's time we quit playing defense and start playing offense; to quit letting our circumstances get between us and God and let God get between us and our circumstances.

So, here's my encouragement for you today: Let faith arise in your heart and declare God's Word over your life no matter what you are facing. When you begin to speak TO your mountain, TO your situations, and you are fully persuaded, fully believing that the mountain has got to go, something supernatural happens—that mountain has to move out of your way! Remember, God is a faithful God, but we have to follow His instructions and do things HIS way. When you do things God's way, He always leads you in the way of victory!

Speak to your mountain.

How did today's principle impact you?

_____

_____

_____

_____

_____

Is this something you practice consistently, or is there any area that needs improvement?

_____

_____

_____

_____

How can you take today's principle and apply it to your daily routine?

_____

_____

_____

_____

Prayer enlisting the Lord's help to grow in this discipline

_____

_____

_____

_____

_____

List five things you are grateful for in the last 24 hours

1._____
2._____
3._____
4._____
5._____

List five dreams or goals that you are expecting to happen

1._____
2._____
3._____
4._____
5._____

List your top five "daily affirmations" based on the Word, starting with "I Am....."

1._____
2._____
3._____
4._____
5._____

NOTES

_____
_____
_____
_____
_____
_____
_____
_____
_____
_____
_____
_____
_____
_____
_____
_____

Day 17

Set Your Mind - Then Align Your Heart, Mind and Mouth

COLOSSIANS 3:2 - "SET your mind on things above, not on earth."

So today our principle is a very powerful combination! While these principles are all good separately, TOGETHER they are amazingly powerful! The phrase "set your mind" means **you are determined to do whatever "IT" is!** This goes all the way back to Day 2, "If the Bible says it, I believe it," when we talked about how you just resolve to believe what God says, no deterring. If He said it, I just believe it! I'm determined that He's got me, and I'm going to be still and remind myself who HE is and trust wholeheartedly in Him. I make the choice not to let fear dictate my life. On Day 13 we talked about how Jesus disarms fear and how there is no reason to fear if the Spirit is within us, so take heart, things will get better soon.

When you set your mind on things above, you reorient your thinking and living to revolve around God and His Kingdom and doing things HIS way! You make HIM priority in your life and always put HIM first.

Matthew 6:33 says, *"Seek ye first the Kingdom of God, then all these things will be added to you."*

Our key verse today is Colossians 3:2, *"Set your mind on things above, not on earth."*

You see, many people want to walk in victory everyday, but they don't want to do it God's way! And that mindset is really a 50/50 crap shoot—it's risky—it may or may not happen. And lots of times when things don't go well, because they haven't put any of these principles in place, they end up depressed, lonely, sad, and even bitter.

So, today, I encourage you to SET YOUR MIND! Be determined to do it God's way! His ways are higher, and they are better than anything we could think of ourselves. THEN, make sure these other principles are in place. It makes all the difference in the world when we align our heart (desire/emotion), mind (focus/resolve), and our mouth (words - God's Words).

It's a powerful combination that will produce SUPERNATURAL results! Have a blessed day as you SET YOUR MIND and align your heart, mind, and mouth!

How did today's principle impact you?

_____

_____

_____

_____

_____

Is this something you practice consistently, or is there any area that needs improvement?

_____

_____

_____

_____

How can you take today's principle and apply it to your daily routine?

_____

_____

_____

_____

Prayer enlisting the Lord's help to grow in this discipline

_____

_____

_____

_____

_____

List five things you are grateful for in the last 24 hours

1._____
2._____
3._____
4._____
5._____

List five dreams or goals that you are expecting to happen

1._____
2._____
3._____
4._____
5._____

List your top five "daily affirmations" based on the Word, starting with "I Am....."

1._____
2._____
3._____
4._____
5._____

NOTES

Day 18

God is Always Speaking - Listen for Him

I SAMUEL 3:10, NLT: "And Samuel replied, 'Speak, your servant is listening.'"

Today we have another really good principle— "God is always speaking. Listen for Him." It's actually going to be two parts, so we will finish it up tomorrow. For today, we are going to read a passage out of the Bible that tells an amazing story. You may have heard it or read it before, but for now, let's look at it together in 1 Samuel 3:1-20.

This is the story about Samuel and Eli. First, a little background: Eli is an older priest at the time of this writing, and Samuel is a young boy. Let's start at verse 1 in The New Living Translation:

Meanwhile, the boy Samuel served the Lord by assisting Eli. Now, in those days, messages from the Lord were very rare, and visions were quite uncommon. One night, Eli, who was almost blind by now, had gone to bed. The lamp of God had not yet gone out, and Samuel was sleeping in the tabernacle near the Arc of God. Suddenly the Lord called out Samuel. "Yes", Samuel replied, "what is it?" He got up and ran to Eli." Here I am. Did you call me?" "I didn't call you". Eli replied, "go back to bed." So he did. Then the Lord called out again, "Samuel!" Again, Samuel got up and he went to Eli. "Here I am. Did you call me?" "I didn't call you, my son", Eli said. "Go back to bed." Samuel did not yet know the Lord because he had never had a message from the Lord before. So the Lord called a third time, and once more, Samuel got up and went to Eli. "Here I am. Did you call me?" Then Eli realized it was the Lord who was calling the boy. So he said to Samuel, "Go and lie down again, and if someone calls again, say speak Lord, your servant is listening." So Samuel went back to bed and the Lord came and called as before. "Samuel, Samuel!", and Samuel replied, "speak Lord, your servant is listening."

Alright, I just want you to mull around that story today because I think a lot of times God calls us and He's saying (and I'll insert my own name here), "Terri, Terri!" and either I'm just not paying attention, or I'm too busy, or I'm very distracted, and I miss it. I miss His voice! I miss Him calling me. Or maybe I just THINK I heard something—I just don't know. Maybe I run in the wrong direction thinking I heard something from another source. And I know I'm not the only one that finds themselves in this position. So today I want you to think about this story, and I want you to think about some factors that hinder us, that hinder YOU, from hearing the voice of God. Because as today's principle says, "God is always speaking." We just have to LISTEN for Him!

That is my challenge to you today. He's speaking to you, and I want you to quiet yourself, limit the distractions, and listen for the next 24 hours. Be intentional. Be purposeful. Pay attention. Be still. We have to find some quiet time. Sometimes we crowd ourselves with so much stuff—a long "to do" list—that we can't hear what He's trying to say to us or what He's trying to show us. So, I'm going to tell you like Eli told Samuel, go back to bed (not literally, but get somewhere that you can be still before the Lord), and when you hear the voice speak, position yourself and say, "Speak, Lord. Your servant is listening."

Did you see what you must do? Position yourself! That's tomorrow's principle. Position yourself and say, "Speak Lord, your servant is listening!" And I'm telling you—He's going to talk to you. He's going to reveal some things to you. If you position yourself and *listen* for Him, He WILL speak to you!

How did today's principle impact you?

_____

_____

_____

Is this something you practice consistently, or is there any area that needs improvement?

_____

_____

_____

How can you take today's principle and apply it to your daily routine?

_____

_____

_____

_____

_____

Prayer enlisting the Lord's help to grow in this discipline

_____

_____

_____

_____

_____

List five things you are grateful for in the last 24 hours

1._____
2._____
3._____
4._____
5._____

List five dreams or goals that you are expecting to happen

1._____
2._____
3._____
4._____
5._____

List your top five "daily affirmations" based on the Word, starting with "I Am....."

1._____
2._____
3._____
4._____
5._____

NOTES

_____
_____
_____
_____
_____
_____
_____
_____
_____
_____
_____
_____
_____
_____
_____
_____

Day 19

Position Yourself

1 KINGS 19:11, NLT: "Go out and stand before me on the mountain," the Lord told him. And as Elijah stood there, the Lord passed by..."

Today's devotion is a bit longer than the others, but so good— "Position yourself!" We're carrying on from yesterday where Samuel said, *"Speak Lord, your servant is listening."* Our principle yesterday was, "God is always speaking, just listen for Him." And today I want us to go a step further by getting into position to hear God the best way possible. To hear Him as clearly as possible. Sometimes we have to intentionally get in position. To "position oneself" means exactly what you would imagine it to mean—**to occupy a certain space, or to be situated**. There's nothing super deep about that. It is just exactly what you think. Get situated. Occupy. And get ready for whatever it is that's coming.

Let's look at 1 Kings 18 for a little history on the prophet Elijah. Elijah was a great prophet for the Lord and for the people of Israel. In this passage, he was up against 450 false prophets of Baal. To shorten the story, Elijah said, *"Let's see who the one true God is."* Obviously, he knew who it was, but he had to prove to the 450 prophets that his God was the one true God, and they were serving a false God. His proposition to them: *"Let's see whose God can cause fire to come down and burn up this offering."* The false prophets' fire never came. Nothing happened. Not even the hint of a spark. Nothing. Well, as you can already guess, it turned out that Elijah wins. The one true God wins! His God was victorious. God caused the fire to come. Can you imagine the chatter among the false prophets? Just maybe it was something like this: "Ooh, He IS the one true God! Baal didn't listen to the prophets! Maybe Baal ain't real. He fake!" At this point, Elijah takes all of those 450 false prophets down to the river and kills every one of them.

Before we continue with this story, let's look at two other supernatural things that happened here in 1 Kings 18 that vividly show us God was definitely at work in Elijah's life. Following the killing of the 450 false prophets, Elijah predicted a rainstorm—that a heavy rain was coming—although the sky was clear. (Spoiler alert: within no time at all, the rain did come—out of nowhere—from nothing but clear skies!) Elijah tried to warn the King that he had better hurry and go home. All of a sudden in the sky, rain in the size of a man's hand appeared in the clouds. They all started home, and God gave supernatural strength to Elijah and he OUTRAN the King's chariots all the way home—on foot! So, these 3 great things had just happened: Elijah prayed for fire from heaven, and it came; Elijah predicted heavy rain when the skies were clear, and it came; Elijah outran a chariot. Now let's head over to 1 Kings 19 and jump back into the story.

When Jezebel heard what Elijah had done, how he had killed her 450 prophets, she was beside herself and said in verses 1-2 of 1 Kings 19, *"May the gods strike me and even kill me if by this time tomorrow I have not killed you (Ellijah) as you have killed them.*"Now remember, he had just defeated and killed 450 false prophets. But this ONE woman, Jezebel, had some kind of power over him because those words sent him running for his life. Literally! The scriptures say that Elijah *"was afraid and fled for his life."* Really? He runs straightway to the wilderness, and he hides in a cave.

See if you don't find yourself here sometimes. You have an incredible encounter with God, you're on top of the mountain, but then life happens—you get an unexpected health report, or something happens, something comes to you, you get bad news of something—and it sends you running. It sends you to your bed, it depletes your appetite. Your emotions are everywhere. This is Elijah. He runs. He goes and finds a tree, and he just plops down under it, to sleep and starve. That's his version of going to bed and not eating. His energy is depleted. He's exhausted. He has no appetite. It would be like us being in bed, pulling the covers over our head and not coming out, even for food. We're not hungry. We don't want to talk to anybody. We isolate ourselves. This is exactly what Elijah did—right after he had supernatural victories in the face of his enemies!

Let's pick back up with the story in 1 Kings 19. Here's what happens. The angel of the Lord comes to him and wakes him up. *"Elijah, get up. You need to eat."* Supernaturally, bread and water appeared. He needs to eat. He's going to need strength for what's coming. Well, he did. He was obedient. But then immediately he went right back to sleep again. So basically, he didn't get out of bed. He stayed in bed with his head covered. And the angel says, *"Elijah, get up. Eat some more. You're going to need more strength."* Again, he was obedient, and he got up and ate. After he got up the second time, God grabbed his attention. And here's where I want us to key in, 1 Kings 19:11.

In this verse, the Lord tells him to go out and stand before Him on the mountain. This verse got me thinking! I think the Lord was saying here, "Elijah! get up and go position yourself. I'm going to talk to you, and I need you to go and position yourself." I think He says that to us sometimes as well! "Get up! Get up from bed. Get up off of the floor. Get out of that chair. Go position yourself. Stand on the mountain." And thankfully Elijah did! And as he stood there, here's what it says happened (and I'm going to paraphrase this), *"The Lord passed by and a mighty windstorm came."* Or one translation says a hurricane. *"But the Lord was not in the windstorm. He was not in the hurricane."* Those are huge deals! One would think obviously that must be God. But it wasn't. *"After the windstorm came an earthquake."* Okay, this has got to be it. God's booming voice in the earthquake. This is how He's going to speak to me; I just know it! *"But the Lord wasn't in the earthquake. After the earthquake, a fire."* Okay, yeah, God appears in fire. Surely, He will speak to me from the fire. That's got to be Him. But the Lord wasn't in the fire. And it says, *"After the fire, there was the sound of a gentle whisper."* A gentle whisper. *"And when Elijah heard it, he wrapped his face in his coat, or his cloak, and then he went from the top of the mountain and stood back at the entrance of the cave."*

So, I am reading that he **repositioned** himself again. He heard God's voice on the mountain top as it came in a gentle whisper. He heard it because he was obedient and intentional. He obeyed God and positioned himself. But look what happens AFTER He heard God's voice in the gentle whisper. He went and repositioned himself *again* in front of the mouth of the cave! And the scripture continues saying that *"God came and spoke to him and gave him the instructions that he needed."* He told him where to go and what he was to do. Elijah went and did what God told him to do. He had his answer, he came out of "hiding" and God was with him.

So, my friend, wherever you are today, position yourself! Maybe you need to get up and go stand on "the mountain." Then reposition yourself back to "the cave." Listen for that still small voice. He is always speaking, but we miss Him sometimes because we thought for sure He'd speak from the hurricane, or the earthquake or even the fire. Get in position and listen for Him in the gentle whisper. He wants to speak to you.

How did today's principle impact you?

_____

_____

_____

Is this something you practice consistently, or is there any area that needs improvement?

_____

_____

_____

_____

How can you take today's principle and apply it to your daily routine?

_____

_____

_____

_____

Prayer enlisting the Lord's help to grow in this discipline

_____

_____

_____

_____

List five things you are grateful for in the last 24 hours

1._____
2._____
3._____
4._____
5._____

List five dreams or goals that you are expecting to happen

1._____
2._____
3._____
4._____
5._____

List your top five "daily affirmations" based on the Word, starting with "I Am....."

1._____
2._____
3._____
4._____
5._____

NOTES

Day 20

Pray without Ceasing

1 THESSALONIANS 5:16-18, NLT - "Always be joyful. Never stop praying. Be thankful in all circumstances, for this is God's will for you who belong to Christ Jesus."

At our church, you will often hear us say, "Prayer is not the only thing you can do; it is the best thing you can do." And what a true statement this is! Over the past two days, we've talked about listening for God's voice and positioning ourselves so that we can hear Him. Those principles make up one aspect of prayer. You all know that prayer is 2-way communication, with us hearing from God being one way, the other being us talking to God! Simply put, prayer is us talking to God, and us hearing from God!

Look at our key verse for today: 1 Thessalonians 5:16-18, NLT— *"Always be joyful. Never stop praying. Be thankful in all circumstances, for this is God's will for you who belong to Christ Jesus."*

In the New King James Version, verse 17 ("Never stop praying.") is actually translated as today's principle: **"Pray without Ceasing."** The word cease means **to stop or end**. God is telling us that His will for us who belong to Jesus is to not stop praying! Prayer is a vital aspect of our Christian lives, and we should not take it lightly! Prayer is a way for us to spend time with God. Like any relationship, when you don't spend time with the other person, the relationship is going to suffer. Prayer is simply communicating with God. Through prayer, we are able to connect with God and align our hearts with His.

Philippians 4:6-7, NLT - *"Don't worry about anything; instead, pray about everything. Tell God what you need, and thank him for all he has done. Then you will experience God's peace, which exceeds anything we can understand. His peace will guard your hearts and minds as you live in Christ Jesus."*

Let me close today by sharing more benefits that we get from praying! Prayer helps us focus, to STAY HOPEFUL (already talked about that one too...how do people do it without the hope Jesus gives us?). We find comfort and peace. Prayer gives us STRENGTH; keeps our minds and thoughts clear; and we receive GUIDANCE and SUPPORT! There's more! These are just a few!

Make sure you're back for tomorrow's principle as we talk more on prayer—the benefits of praying in the Spirit—and how my husband fought and battled using PRAYER AS HIS WEAPON during his health challenge at the end of 2023! It's going to be good! Make today a great day and pray all throughout the day! Never stop praying!

How did today's principle impact you?

_____

_____

_____

_____

_____

Is this something you practice consistently, or is there any area that needs improvement?

_____

_____

_____

_____

How can you take today's principle and apply it to your daily routine?

_____

_____

_____

_____

Prayer enlisting the Lord's help to grow in this discipline

_____

_____

_____

_____

List five things you are grateful for in the last 24 hours

1._____

2._____

3._____

4._____

5._____

List five dreams or goals that you are expecting to happen

1._____

2._____

3._____

4._____

5._____

List your top five "daily affirmations" based on the Word, starting with "I Am....."

1._____

2._____

3._____

4._____

5._____

NOTES

Day 21

Pray in the Spirit - Pray in Tongues

ROMANS 8:26, ESV - "Likewise the Spirit helps us in our weakness for we do not know what to pray as we ought, but the Spirit himself intercedes for us with groanings too deep for words."

Today's principle continues with the principle of prayer, but in a different vein. Allow me to set the stage by reading a few scriptures before we jump into how this principle today literally saved my husband's life when he went through a very serious health battle at the end of 2023. The principle today is **"Pray in the Spirit, Pray in tongues."** I know people have different beliefs when it comes to the Holy Spirit and speaking in tongues but hang in there with me. At least listen to our story! And yes, it's a long one today—it's personal.

I just want to share some scriptures that I'm basing my conviction on and then tell you the part of the story where I know this principle saved Brent's life. We see in Acts 1 that Jesus has been resurrected and is now spending some time with the disciples. He tells them that they are not to leave Jerusalem or go anywhere because the Father is going to send them the gift of the Holy Spirit, and they are soon going to be "baptized" with this gift.

Let's look at Acts 2:1-4, *"When the day of Pentecost came, when that promised day came, they were all together and the Holy Spirit came from heaven. It was the sound of a mighty rushing wind. It filled the entire house where they were sitting, divided tongues of fire appeared to them and rested on each one of them, and they were all filled with the Holy Spirit and began to speak in other tongues as the Spirit gave them utterance."* In the New Living Translation, verse 4 says, *"...and everyone present was filled with the Holy Spirit and began speaking in other languages as the Holy Spirit gave them this ability."* Jump over to Romans 8:26-28 and let's look at this passage. First here is verse 26, our key verse today, *"Likewise the Spirit helps us in our weakness for we do not know what to pray as we ought, but the Spirit himself intercedes for us with groanings too deep for words."*

What I found interesting is we're all familiar with the verse that is two doors down, Romans 8:28, *"But we know that all things work together for good to those who love Jesus."* But notice verses 26 and 27 that precede verse 28! Let's read the three together in The Voice Translation so you have a little bit more context. *"A similar thing happens when we pray. We are weak and don't know how to pray. So the Spirit steps in and articulates prayers for us with groaning too profound for words. Don't you know that He who pursues and explores the human heart intimately knows the Spirit's mind because He pleads to God for His saints to align their lives with the will of God?"* And THEN it says in verse 28, *"We are confident that God is able to orchestrate everything to work towards something good and beautiful when we love Him and accept His invitation to live according to His plan."*

Okay, one more verse and then I'm going to jump into parts of our story. 1 Corinthians 14:2 in The Voice says, *"You see, a person speaking in an unknown language is not addressing the church because he is really addressing God—those who overhear don't understand because he is speaking in the Spirit the depths of the mysteries of the Lord."* And in the English Standard Version, it says, *"For one who speaks in a tongue speaks not to men but to God; for no one understands him, but he utters mysteries in the Spirit."*

One night in October 2023, my husband had an incident during the night. It happened to be on a night that I was sick. He was awakened in the middle of the night, jumped out of bed, disoriented, flung his arms all around, hit the light switch, turned the light on and turned the fan off. Very unexpected. Very chaotic. He didn't know what was happening. Feeling poorly myself with flu-like symptoms, I didn't know what was happening. All I know is after the initial jolt out of bed, he turned the fan back on and turned the light off, and he paced for hours in that bedroom. In the dark. Praying.

We were on a trip, so we were staying in an Airbnb with four other families. He paced back and forth in the room, back and forth, and he said, "Terri, just pray". Okay, I'm in bed not feeling well and all I could do was just say the name of Jesus. "Jesus, Jesus, Jesus." Over and over. I could only speak the name of Jesus over Brent. He tried to tell me what was happening, but he had a hard time explaining what he was feeling in his body. A trembling. A shaking. A tingling. His hands and arms were tingling and numb, his legs, all of his extremities. His feet were numb. This was what was happening on the inside, but you couldn't see it on the outside. So, he got back in bed, and all I know is for hours he just prayed. And probably 90% of that was praying in the Spirit. He didn't know what else to say. I mean, what can you say for hours except "God heal me. God heal me! God, what's going on? Heal me." He prayed in his prayer language, in tongues, and I was just saying the name of Jesus, and as he was praying in his prayer language, he said he would feel it break. He eventually fell back asleep, and we finished our trip.

That same thing happened again in November. We were on a cruise in the middle of the Caribbean ocean. Now Brent kept all this pretty private, even from me. He never would just tell me what he was feeling unless it was really bad. And then he would go into detail. Other than that, he and God were taking care of this. So, this whole time, I didn't realize the severity of what was going on inside of him and that makes me want to cry right now. But that night on the cruise ship, he literally had to get out of bed to pace and pray. He went out on our little balcony. He came back in and got fully dressed. This was two or three in the morning. He said, "I'm going walking." Okay, I'm dead asleep and I didn't realize he's having serious issues. But later he tells me that he seriously thought, *"I think I might be dying."* The first time it happened he had also thought that same thing, *"I think I need to go to the hospital. Something's wrong. I might be dying."* Here he is again in November, in the middle of the ocean, on a ship where the medical facilities he may need were not even accessible to us. As he went to walk and pray, he could barely go up a couple of flights of stairs. Once he reached the top of the stairs, he was gasping for air, and again thought, *"I might die."* He actually thought he may be having a heart attack. *"I think I'm going to die."* So, he just began praying in the spirit. And later he said, "I felt it break." He was able to come back to bed. And we finished the cruise and everything was good.

A similar event happened one other time at our house, following the cruise, at the end of November. One night I got up to go check on him because he hadn't been sleeping much these months. This particular night I found him in the living room. Pacing and praying. He had done that several times before, so I was going back to bed but instead, he told me he needed me in there with him to pray. At this point, I knew something terrible was going on. That night he probably prayed in the Spirit for six hours or more. It was an all-nighter. I managed to pray for two or three hours with him, praying in the Spirit, praying in our prayer language or tongues, whatever you want to call it. I would hear him praying and he would break off in English, and he would declare the things he was determined to see and do: *I will go skiing in January with my family. I will have a good Christmas. I will live to see my grandkids grow up and be old.* I was thinking, of course, you are going to do all those things! I didn't realize that he was fighting other thoughts: *I think I might die. Do I need to go to the hospital?* And we just kept praying in the Spirit. One more side note: he told me several times he would **will himself** to go into his bathroom and look at himself in the mirror and speak scriptures to himself. He said, *"You will live and not die and live to tell the works of the Lord." "No weapon formed against you will prosper."* "I command my body to line up with the Word of God." He could do this because he had put The Word in himself, and he was speaking to his mountain. Remember that principle? He was speaking God's Word and willing himself to live. He had told me that he thought his mind was going to snap many times and that he was going to die.

Honestly, I didn't realize the depth of all of that until after the fact. At the beginning of this ordeal, he did not know if it was spiritual or physical, because every time with fervent prayer, it would eventually break and seem to go away (until the next night—always at night, never in the daytime). He was just so exhausted and worn out from not sleeping the night before. It was just a vicious cycle. But he thought, "I better seek medical help and get checked out." He originally thought it was a spiritual attack because it would break every time he would **pray in the Spirit**. After a few hours, he would feel it loosen. Multiple tests came back and showed everything looked good—EKG, echocardiogram, stress test, etc. We thought it was sleep apnea and took action for that, but nothing really changed. He had had a nuclear stress test that showed something, so at the urging of his cardiologist he underwent an arteriogram. His widowmaker (the largest artery in your heart, the LAD artery) was 100% blocked. He, in fact, could have (and maybe in the natural realm should have) died. But God! But God gave us a powerful heavenly language that only the Holy Spirit knew what and how to pray for in this situation. Those nights that he was praying in the Spirit, he didn't know what was happening. He didn't know to ask specifically that God would unclog his main artery so that he could live. He didn't even know he had a heart problem! What he did was he prayed in the Spirit, because the Holy Spirit KNEW exactly what needed to be said! And this brings us full circle back to our key verse which says, "*...and the Spirit articulates our prayers, and He goes to God because He knows the heart of God, and He's aligning our heart and our will with what God's will is for us...*"

So, now, when anyone ever asks me the importance of praying in the Spirit, I will tell them, "It may be the only thing that can save your life." It is for sure what saved my husband's life. I know the Holy Spirit was sitting there interceding for Brent at those very moments, saying, "God, you see what's going on? His artery is blocked. He doesn't know, but his widowmaker is blocked. It could take his life. And I'm asking you, God,

I'm asking you, Jesus to unplug, to unclog that artery. Let him get the help so they can fix it." And while Brent was just praying in the Spirit, the Holy Spirit was pinpointing that issue over and over and over, and he's still alive today because of the power of praying in the Spirit. The Holy Spirit took his need to the Lord. He articulated those prayers beautifully. And now my husband is clear!

And I just want you to know that I one-hundred-percent give God all the credit, all the glory, all the praise for Brent's miraculous healing. The finding, the fixing, and now the living. We're going to live to be old together, to see our grandkids grow up. I will never ever doubt the role the Holy Spirit had in this process. The fact is that this prayer language is a gift from God, freely given to all who believe, and that gift saved Brent's life. I will not cease to testify to the power of having your heavenly language. And I do realize not everyone here has their prayer language. What I would say to you is maybe go back to the beginning of this with all the scriptures and do a little research. And all I say is, just be open. This is a gift. It is a gift to everyone who believes. And I'm just asking you, would you be open? Just be open to the Lord and say, *"God, if this is a gift for me and I'm missing out, I want the gift. I want the free gift. Please give me everything You've got!"* And I promise you that He will speak to you. He'll move on you, and He'll open your heart and your eyes.

Yeah, it's mysterious. But it's only something that we do through the ability of the Holy Spirit. *"...but the Spirit himself intercedes for us with groanings too deep for words."* God gives us this so we can have the power to walk through what we just walked through, and then to be witnesses of Jesus to everyone around us. And that is just one extra, very vital, important way to live in victory every day. Pray in the Spirit. Pray in tongues.

How did today's principle impact you?

_____

_____

_____

_____

Is this something you practice consistently, or is there any area that needs improvement?

_____

_____

_____

_____

How can you take today's principle and apply it to your daily routine?

_____

_____

_____

_____

Prayer enlisting the Lord's help to grow in this discipline

_____

_____

_____

_____

List five things you are grateful for in the last 24 hours

1._____

2._____

3._____

4._____

5._____

List five dreams or goals that you are expecting to happen

1._____

2._____

3._____

4._____

5._____

List your top five "daily affirmations" based on the Word, starting with "I Am....."

1._____

2._____

3._____

4._____

5._____

List five things you are grateful for in the last 24 hours

List intentions or goals that you are hoping for... to happen

List your top five daily affirmations based on the Word starting with
"I am:"

NOTES

Day 22

Be Grateful - Be Thankful

I Thessalonians 5:18, NLT - "Be thankful in all circumstances, for this is God's will for you who belong to Christ Jesus."

The principle today is a good one: "Be grateful, Be thankful." I want to read several scriptures, some of which I have already covered in past lessons. Sometimes they just overlap. And I just think when scriptures overlap like this for multiple principles, they must be pretty important. So, let's just decide, resolve that we are going to take these scriptures, some of which are very familiar to us, and we're going to put them into practice every single day so that we can live in victory as best as we possibly can.

Look at Philippians 4. I would encourage you at some point to read through this chapter. I'm going to start at verse 10 but let me set this up for you a little bit. Paul is the author of this book and here he's talking to the believers at Philippi. He's saying in verse 10, *"How I praise the Lord that you are concerned for me, but you just didn't have the chance to help me. Not that I was ever in need, for I have learned to be content with whatever I have.*

I know how to live on almost nothing or with everything. I have learned the secret of living in every situation, whether it is with a full stomach or empty, with plenty or little. " And obviously verse 13 is one you've heard before but notice the timing of when it appears.

It says, *"For I can do everything through Christ who gives me strength."* Again, this is a scripture we quote often, but did we even look to see what it was that he was saying right before he wrote this verse? He was saying that I've been in situations where I've had EVERYTHING and where I've had NOTHING! So, whether Paul had a lot or a little, whether he was full or hungry, he learned to be content. And THEN he says, *"For I can do everything through Christ who gives me strength."* In The Voice Translation, here's what verses 11-13 tell us. *"I'm not saying this because I'm in need. I have learned to be content in whatever circumstances. For I know how to survive in tight situations, and I know how to enjoy having plenty. In fact, I've learned to face any circumstance, fed or hungry, with or without. I can be content in any and every situation, through the Anointed One, who is my power and my strength."*

Y'all! Paul learned to be content BECAUSE he had the hope and the promise that with God and through Jesus Christ, he could face ANY-THING! He had the strength to get through anything. That is being grateful. Even when we wish the situation was different, we still can be grateful for what God has done for us and what he is doing for us in our life.

Let's close out today with a little bit of the Bible on thankfulness. Let's look at 1 Thessalonians 5:18, our key verse for today. It says, *"Give thanks in all circumstances, for this is God's will for you in Christ Jesus."* He didn't say be thankful only when things are going well. He says, be thankful in whatever it is. And just like Paul said, whatever state I find myself in I'm going to be content, grateful, and thankful.

God said, *"This is my will for you: to be thankful no matter what your circumstance."* And then in Philippians 4:6-7 (we talked about this the other day) it says, *"Do not be anxious about anything, but in every situation* <u>*by prayer and petition with thanksgiving,*</u> *present your requests to God."* So, when you go to pray and you're stretching and you're deepening your prayer life, put a little thanksgiving in there. Paul says, with THANKS-GIVING, present your requests to God!

We have so much to be thankful for. Psalm 100:4 says, *"Enter His gates with thanksgiving, And into His courts with praise. Be thankful to Him, and bless His name."* WHY? *"Because the LORD is good; His mercy is everlasting, And His truth endures to all generations."* So, friends, when we come to God we have so many reasons to be thankful. Jesus is the greatest of those reasons. And, bringing thankfulness, gratitude, and praise to God is a way for us to worship Him.

Be grateful. Be thankful.

How did today's principle impact you?

_____

_____

_____

_____

Is this something you practice consistently, or is there any area that needs improvement?

_____

_____

_____

_____

How can you take today's principle and apply it to your daily routine?

_____

_____

_____

_____

Prayer enlisting the Lord's help to grow in this discipline

_____

_____

_____

_____

_____

List five things you are grateful for in the last 24 hours

1._____

2._____

3._____

4._____

5._____

List five dreams or goals that you are expecting to happen

1._____

2._____

3._____

4._____

5._____

List your top five "daily affirmations" based on the Word, starting with "I Am....."

1._____

2._____

3._____

4._____

5._____

NOTES

Day 23

You Reap What You Sow - Be Generous

TODAY'S PRINCIPLE IS "YOU reap what you sow, so be generous!" Let's look at several scriptures today. They will do most of the talking for us, and they are really good—I think you'll like them! Let's begin with our key verse for today, Galatians 6:7-9:

Galatians 6:7-9, The Voice - *"Make no mistake: God can't be mocked. What you give is what you get. What you sow, you harvest. Those who sow seeds into their flesh will only harvest destruction from their sinful nature. But those who sow seeds into the Spirit shall harvest everlasting life from the Spirit. May we never tire of doing what is good and right before our Lord because in His season we shall bring in a great harvest if we can just persist."*

2 Corinthians 9:6, NLT - *"Remember this—a farmer who plants only a few seeds will get a small crop. But the one who plants generously will get a generous crop."*

2 Corinthians 9:6, The Voice - *"But I will say this to encourage your generosity: the one who plants little harvests little, and the one who plants plenty harvests plenty."*

Genesis 8:22, The Voice - *"As long as the earth endures (or remains), nothing will put a stop to planting and harvest..."* (Some translations read seedtime and harvest.)

This is a principle that will ALWAYS exist! Genesis 8 says so! *"As long as the earth remains, there will ALWAYS be seedtime, and harvest."* What each of us does with our resources, and our time, is completely up to us! Most of us do think in terms of money when thinking of sowing and reaping, and harvests, but look—this applies to everything! Our time, our kindness, our help, our money, our talents. If we invest/plant/sow little, then that's what we will reap/get back in return. Again, we get to choose how "generous" we are!

And YES! Part of sowing/reaping involves money! Be "open-handed" towards God with your finances! (Tithing is our principle for tomorrow.) What you sow, you will reap!

So, I just want to encourage you today to incorporate this principle in your life every day! And let it be said of you, "Because I am a habitual/continuous sower, I will be a habitual/continual reaper!"

You reap what you sow, so be generous.

How did today's principle impact you?

_____

_____

_____

_____

Is this something you practice consistently, or is there any area that needs improvement?

_____

_____

_____

_____

How can you take today's principle and apply it to your daily routine?

_____

_____

_____

_____

Prayer enlisting the Lord's help to grow in this discipline

_____

_____

_____

_____

List five things you are grateful for in the last 24 hours

1._____
2._____
3._____
4._____
5._____

List five dreams or goals that you are expecting to happen

1._____
2._____
3._____
4._____
5._____

List your top five "daily affirmations" based on the Word, starting with "I Am....."

1._____
2._____
3._____
4._____
5._____

NOTES

Day 24

Be a Tither

MALACHI 3:10-12, NLT - *"'Bring all the tithes into the storehouse so there will be enough food in my Temple. If you do,' says the Lord of Heaven's Armies, 'I will open the windows of heaven for you. I will pour out a blessing so great you won't have enough room to take it in! Try it! Put me to the test! Your crops will be abundant, for I will guard them from insects and disease. Your grapes will not fall from the vine before they are ripe,' says the Lord of Heaven's Armies. 'Then all nations will call you blessed, for your land will be such a delight,' says the Lord of Heaven's Armies."*

Let's start at the very beginning, with the FIRST FAMILY. This story is found in Genesis 4:2-5, NLT - *"Abel became a shepherd, while Cain cultivated the ground. When it was time for the harvest, Cain presented some of his crops as a gift to the Lord. Abel also brought a gift—the best portions of the firstborn lambs from his flock. The Lord accepted Abel and his gift, but he did not accept Cain and his gift."*

While Abel gave the best he could, a firstborn lamb from his flock, Cain gave SOME of his crops, possibly a mere "garden variety" of assorted produce. You see, tithing isn't just a matter of the pocketbook. It is a matter of the heart.

Genesis 14:19-20, NLT - *"Melchizedek (the High Priest at the time) blessed Abram with this blessing: 'Blessed be Abram by God Most High, Creator of heaven and earth. And blessed be God Most High, who has defeated your enemies for you.' Then Abram gave Melchizedek a tenth of all the goods he had recovered."*

And now WE get to enjoy even greater blessings through our tithing today, because we bring our tithes to our High Priest—Jesus—who is greater than Melchizedek or any other Old Covenant priest! We certainly don't do it just for the blessings, but it's such a nice benefit when we do things God's way. In case you are new to the tithing principle, it is simply a tenth of your earnings that you set aside first and give to God! Thus, first fruits. When you do this principle of tithing, it unlocks a multitude of blessings for you!

The Bible is very clear in Leviticus 27:30 - *"A tenth of the produce of the land, whether grain or fruit, is the Lord's, and is HOLY. AND, above all else, it gives HONOR to God!"*

Proverbs 3:9-10 - *"Honor the Lord with your possessions (wealth), with the first fruits of all your increase (Honor Him with the best of what you make) so your barns will be filled with plenty, and your vats will overflow with new wine (That way you will prosper to the fullest and have plenty of food to eat and wine to drink.)."*

In closing, let's look at a popular scripture passage on tithing, and obviously our key verses today: Malachi 3:10-12, NLT - *"Bring all the tithes into the storehouse so there will be enough food in my Temple. If you do,' says the Lord of Heaven's Armies, 'I will open the windows of heaven for you. I will pour out a blessing so great you won't have enough room to take it in! Try it! Put me to the test! Your crops will be abundant, for I will guard them from insects and disease. Your grapes will not fall from the vine before they are ripe,' says the Lord of Heaven's Armies. 'Then all nations will call you blessed, for your land will be such a delight,' says the Lord of Heaven's Armies."*

How true these verses are! I mean, look at what God says HE will do in our lives if we are obedient to being a tither! It absolutely works—I can attest to that! And even God Himself says here, *"Put me to the test!"* Take Him up on it and see what He will do for you!

Just like when we talked about receiving our prayer language the other day, if you aren't a tither, talk to God about it! Be open and willing to hear what He has to say to you about this principle! You will NEVER EVER go wrong with cheerfully bringing your tithe to God! It is such an honor and privilege to respect, revere, and worship our Provider with such a small gift as the tithe—ten percent.

Be a tither.

How did today's principle impact you?

_____

_____

_____

_____

Is this something you practice consistently, or is there any area that needs improvement?

_____

_____

_____

How can you take today's principle and apply it to your daily routine?

_____

_____

_____

Prayer enlisting the Lord's help to grow in this discipline

_____

_____

_____

_____

List five things you are grateful for in the last 24 hours

1._____
2._____
3._____
4._____
5._____

List five dreams or goals that you are expecting to happen

1._____
2._____
3._____
4._____
5._____

List your top five "daily affirmations" based on the Word, starting with "I Am....."

1._____
2._____
3._____
4._____
5._____

NOTES

_____
_____
_____
_____
_____
_____
_____
_____
_____
_____
_____
_____
_____
_____
_____
_____

Day 25

Integrity Matters

PROVERBS 21:3, NLT - *"The Lord is more pleased when we do what is right and just than when we offer him sacrifices."*

Why this? Why is integrity considered a principle that should specifically be a daily part of our faith journey to walking in victory every day? Integrity as defined in the dictionary is: **adherence to moral and ethical principles; soundness of moral character; honesty.**

The Bible defines integrity as **including moral uprightness, honesty and steadfast commitment to righteousness.** And look at this: the biblical understanding of integrity is rooted in a deep sense of adherence to God's commandments as well as a sincere dedication to living a life aligned with divine principles. OR, in other words, aligned to doing it God's way! Kingdom Living (God's way of living), EVERY DAY!

Integrity is adhering to these moral/ethical principles—God's commandments—whether you are surrounded by people, or whether you're alone. This means doing the right thing when no one is around, *because it's the right thing to do!* Being who God calls you to be both in public and in private. Integrity is also doing the right thing when it's not easy, or cool, but you know it's the right thing to do, so you do it! And I caution you, that the strength of our integrity is often tested when we are at our weakest!!

You see, integrity reflects God's character. 2 Timothy 2:13, NLT - *"If we are unfaithful, he remains faithful, for he cannot deny who He is."*

Benefits of Integrity:

1. Integrity grants favor. Rahab received favor even though her people were destroyed because she did what was acceptable (right) to God. (You can read more on Rahab in Joshua chapters 2 and 6.) Look at our key verse for today: Proverbs 21:3 - *"To do what is right and just is more acceptable to the Lord than sacrifice."*

2. Integrity gives guidance. Proverbs 11:3 - *"The integrity of the upright guides them, but the unfaithful are destroyed by their duplicity."* (Duplicity = contradictory doubleness of thought, speech, or action—in other words, double-minded or two-faced!)

3. Integrity ensures security. According to the dictionary, security is **the state of being free from danger or threat.** Proverbs 10:9 - *"Whoever walks in integrity walks securely, but whoever takes crooked paths will be found out."*

Never forget to do the right thing. Always. Integrity matters.

How did today's principle impact you?

_____

_____

_____

_____

_____

Is this something you practice consistently, or is there any area that needs improvement?

_____

_____

_____

_____

How can you take today's principle and apply it to your daily routine?

_____

_____

_____

_____

Prayer enlisting the Lord's help to grow in this discipline

_____

_____

_____

_____

_____

List five things you are grateful for in the last 24 hours

1._____

2._____

3._____

4._____

5._____

List five dreams or goals that you are expecting to happen

1._____

2._____

3._____

4._____

5._____

List your top five "daily affirmations" based on the Word, starting with "I Am....."

1._____

2._____

3._____

4._____

5._____

NOTES

Day 26

Forgive

MATTHEW 6:14-15, NLT - "*If you forgive those who sin against you, your heavenly Father will forgive you. But if you refuse to forgive others, your Father will not forgive your sins.*"

Today we have another standalone principle to incorporate into our daily lives to help us live in victory, every single day! Today's principle is to forgive. Yep. Today's principle may be a hard one for most of us, but it is essential to our Christian journey, and it's essential for Kingdom Living Everyday. When we experience hurt or when someone mistreats us, it's very easy for us to harbor bitterness or resentment toward that person. The last thing we want to do is forgive them and move forward as if the situation had never happened. But do you know that being bitter and refusing to forgive will actually disqualify you from receiving God's forgiveness? Before we look at scripture, please hear me. I know this one can be a heavy one, and I don't take lightly any hurt that anyone has ever experienced from another person or a situation.

But with that in mind, let's look at what the Bible says about forgiving in Matthew 6:14-15, which are our key verses for our principle today. *"A person who doesn't forgive others will not be forgiven by God."* The Bible clearly tells us that … *"if we forgive other people when they sin against us, then our heavenly Father will also forgive us. But if we do not forgive others their sins, our father will not forgive our sins."* Those scriptures right there are very powerful, and they are very clear. If we don't forgive those who hurt us, then God won't forgive us.

I know there are many times forgiving someone is difficult. Most of us have been there. We have had situations where we feel like that was "a hard one" to forgive. And some people are still working through their forgiveness. I do believe it is a process. I definitely believe it is. Again though, it's a matter of the heart. Forgiveness doesn't mean that you forget or excuse the harm and hurt that's been done to you, but forgiving a person can help YOU be free from their control. And when it's done right, forgiving can be therapeutic for the person who's been hurt.

Forgiveness leads to better mental, emotional, and even physical health. We all know that unforgiveness and the stress of carrying that load will negatively affect us. It absolutely can and will, most of the time. It affects our physical health. It's hard on the spirit, and it's hard on the body. And I can't help but think of Jesus when he walked on the earth with all the persecution the people threw on Him. All the persecution and the mistreatment that He had coming at Him. That He physically and spiritually felt all of the times He was betrayed. He certainly didn't deserve it from anybody. No, He didn't deserve it, but He took it. Then He turned right around, and He forgave them! Whoever "they" were at the time, He forgave them and then He went a step further. He PRAYED for them! He was able to look beyond the person, the situation and He saw that this was a spiritual battle and behind it was the real enemy, the devil. Satan.

Ephesians 6:12 says, *"For we are not fighting against flesh and blood enemies. It's not people. That's not who we fight against, but against the evil rulers, authorities of the unseen world, against mighty powers in this dark world and against evil spirits in the heavenly places."* Jesus knew this. He knew it was not the person, but it was the spirit driving that person, which is in opposition to God. Jesus knew this, and He forgave. And guess what? He asks and commands us to do the same. Actually, He expects us to do the right thing. He expects us to pray for and to forgive the people that hurt us.

In the Sermon on the Mount in Matthew 5, Jesus says, *"Love your enemies. Bless those who curse you. Pray for those who persecute you, and THEN you'll be blessed."* Those are hard commands to do, but if we can ever tap into them and just say, "Okay God said do it so I'm going to do it HIS way, then we know that what He's got coming for us through that trial and through that experience, through that situation, is going to be so good!" He's going to bring freedom to us! It's going to move us forward—closer to the plan He has for us and will help us to walk in victory every day.

Now let's take it just a tiny bit further as we close out today. In Matthew 18:21-22, Peter wanted clarity on this forgiving subject, so he asked the Lord, *"How many times should I forgive a person? Seven?"* Don't you just love Peter? And Jesus answers him, *"Well, no, not just seven...more like seventy times seven!"*

Peter thinks seven. Jesus says 490. But you know what? He wasn't literally saying to keep count. What He was saying was, we should forgive a limitless number of times. As much as it takes! We forgive. So please hear me. Forgiveness isn't optional. It is mandatory. Forgiveness isn't a feeling. It's a choice. Forgiveness is hard and forgiveness is a process. But God shows us in His Word that with Him all things are possible, and we CAN do this.

Let me pray with you as we close today: "God, I pray for whoever is sitting on the other side of this devotional, reading and hearing this message. God, the hurts, the bitterness, the offense that they are carrying because someone wounded them, they were done wrong and it wasn't fair. But God, you were done wrong and it wasn't fair, and you turned around, and you forgave and you prayed for them. So I pray for whoever's reading this today, God, that you would just surround them with your presence and your peace. That they would feel you with them, and they would know that with God, they can do this. It's definitely a process, but they can do it. So, I bless you today and I pray for strength, wisdom and direction as you move forward with forgiving, however difficult it is. I pray all of this in the name of Jesus. Amen, and Amen."

Forgive.

How did today's principle impact you?

_____

_____

_____

_____

_____

Is this something you practice consistently, or is there any area that needs improvement?

_____

_____

_____

_____

How can you take today's principle and apply it to your daily routine?

_____

_____

_____

_____

Prayer enlisting the Lord's help to grow in this discipline

_____

_____

_____

_____

_____

List five things you are grateful for in the last 24 hours

1._____
2._____
3._____
4._____
5._____

List five dreams or goals that you are expecting to happen

1._____
2._____
3._____
4._____
5._____

List your top five "daily affirmations" based on the Word, starting with "I Am....."

1._____
2._____
3._____
4._____
5._____

NOTES

_____
_____
_____
_____
_____
_____
_____
_____
_____
_____
_____
_____
_____
_____
_____

Day 27

Every Word Matters

PROVERBS 18:21, THE MSG - *"Words kill, words give life. They're either poison or fruit. YOU choose."*

We recently studied how integrity matters, and today our principle is that every WORD matters. Every word you say matters. The words we speak, and our goals and our visions are both topics that are very, very important to me. I am super passionate about them. So, I'm going to spend the next two days on words, then two days on goals and visions and dreaming, and then we will wrap up this month's devotional with a kind of recap and a challenge for you to implement as you move forward. But for today's focus, every word matters.

Our verse for the day is found in Proverbs 18:21, from The Message, *"Words kill, words give life. They're either poison or fruit. YOU choose."* The Message translation always puts it in a way that's kind of in your face. "They're poison or fruit" and you get to choose what they're going to be in your life. Take a minute right now as we're just getting started today and ponder, "What am I saying in my daily routine, in my daily life, just in general? What are the words coming out of my mouth about the situation I'm in right now or the circumstances that surround me?" What is it that keeps coming out of your mouth concerning your situations? How about the people in your life? What are you saying about them?

Words can kill. They can be poisonous. Their fruit can bring death. But also, they can bring LIFE! The power of LIFE is in our words, in our tongue. We can speak life, or we can speak death. The beauty of this is WE get to choose. Some of the ways our words are poisonous are completely obvious, and we certainly know better: gossip, lying, condemning, judging, cursing, putting others down. These are clearly not ways that we're supposed to be speaking! They're not becoming to the Christian life. This behavior is obvious. But there are people that engage in daily negativity that don't even realize how very damaging and poisonous it is because it's not quite as obvious as gossip or lying or cursing! To them the negativity and the complaining are just normal parts of their speech. They don't even think twice about it. It's just how they say what they think without really stopping to think about all the negativity coming out of their mouths (really—from their hearts).

I'm a big fan of affirmations! There's power in affirmations and declarations. But have you ever stopped to think that just as there is great power in positive affirmations, that there is also great power in negative affirmations—when you complain and spew negative words? And that you are actually declaring an affirmation of something that you don't want? Every word matters. People think, oh, I didn't really mean it (I've been there). I think we are all guilty of this. Saying stuff that we didn't literally mean; things said in jest. The sad part is that if we say it consistently enough, our brain thinks that is what it should make happen, so it begins to work as a disadvantage for us.

How much better is it going to be if we choose the fruit and not the poison? When we declare and affirm positive words, the words of God! Yes, positive words, but go beyond that. The more important thing is finding scriptures and saying the WORD of GOD over your life, over your family, over your situation. Every single word matters, and negative words are negative affirmations about something that you don't really want to happen. When you complain about life, your health, your job, your salary, your body, you're just going to attract more to complain about. Complaining is an affirmation!

Here's a good tip to get out of that slump, a scripture for you to pray when you find yourself complaining. Psalm 19:14, (and I have quoted this a lot), *"Let the words of my mouth and the meditation of my heart be acceptable (or pleasing) in your sight, Oh Lord, my rock and my redeemer."* And here's another one that I use in my life. This is where the Holy Spirit comes in and helps us, and I enlist His help often. Psalm 141:3 says, *"Set a guard over my mouth, Lord, keep watch over the door of my lips."* *"Take control of what I say, oh Lord. And guard my lips"* is that same verse in a different translation. *"Set a guard over my mouth"* and *"Take control of what I say."* Many times, I just want to put a big piece of duct tape over my mouth and tell myself to quit talking! Quit talking.

During the time that David wrote this particular psalm, he was running for his life from King Saul and his court. Instead of asking God to kill his enemies (which is what we sometimes think we would like to see happen—for "justice" to come to the other party), he did something else.

He didn't even ask that God deliver him from his enemies. The first thing
he asked was that God would put a guard over his mouth and what he says
because he realized the importance of what was coming out of his mouth.
As he was fleeing for his life, he asked God to take control of his mouth.
Every word matters.

It's also important (and somewhat comforting) to note that David realized he needed assistance in this area of self-control with his mouth. Again,
it is so interesting to me that here he is, running for his life, and instead
of first praying for deliverance or justice or whatever else he might have
wanted to pray, he simply asks God for help with his mouth, his words.

"Holy Spirit, help me. God, help me set a guard over my mouth." More
interesting to note is that these words here, *"set a guard over my mouth,"*
are used in a military sense. A *guard* does not allow anyone in or out of a
walled city during times of war. So how cool is it that when we ask God to
set a guard over our mouth, we can picture Him placing His Spirit there
to MONITOR everything that goes in and out?

Our words, speaking words of life, is a spiritual discipline. But if God
helped David, He will help us too. Every word matters.

How did today's principle impact you?

_____

_____

_____

_____

_____

Is this something you practice consistently, or is there any area that needs improvement?

_____

_____

_____

How can you take today's principle and apply it to your daily routine?

_____

_____

_____

_____

Prayer enlisting the Lord's help to grow in this discipline

_____

_____

_____

_____

List five things you are grateful for in the last 24 hours

1._____
2._____
3._____
4._____
5._____

List five dreams or goals that you are expecting to happen

1._____
2._____
3._____
4._____
5._____

List your top five "daily affirmations" based on the Word, starting with "I Am....."

1._____
2._____
3._____
4._____
5._____

NOTES

_____
_____
_____
_____
_____
_____
_____
_____
_____
_____
_____
_____
_____
_____
_____
_____

Day 28

There is Power in Your Words

MATTHEW 12:37, NLT - *"The words you say will either acquit you or condemn you."*

Today is a carry-over of us talking about words, and how every word matters! Today's principle is about the power in your words. The key verse today, Matthew 12:37 says, *"The words you say will either acquit you or condemn you."* They will either acquit you (free you), or condemn you (bind you up, make guilty). **Your voice is the most influential voice in your life,** so why not use it to help you rather than hinder you? I want to say something that might be a little hard to hear, but it's the truth, and I really want you to take a few minutes today and think about this. It's a statement I've heard several of my mentors reference (including Terri Savelle Foy), and it's so true. "If you want to know where your life is headed, listen to the words that are coming out of your mouth." Let me say that again, "If you want to know where your life is headed, listen to the words coming out of your mouth."

Your words are actually dictating the life you live today. Your words are powerful, and your words spoken over yourself are even more powerful! What is coming out of your mouth has everything to do with what you're experiencing. Let me stop right here and interject this: I'm not saying your words CAUSE everything in your life to happen—because we know that's simply not true. Bad things do happen to good people. Life just isn't fair sometimes because we live in a broken, cursed world. In addition, Jesus told us that in this world we would face troubles. But what I *am* saying is that you have the choice in how you walk through every situation. I have the choice in how I walk through all of my situations, and guess what? Our words play a huge role in this process. Listen to this quote that I really love by Joel Osteen. He says, "Don't use your words to describe your situation. Use your words to change your situation." That could have been in yesterday's devotion as well, because we talked about when we complain and when we're negative, and we think we are just describing whatever it is we're going through. But instead, all we are doing is amplifying it. It's giving the situation more glory than it needs. Don't do it. Just don't do it. Let's not talk about all the bad things, all the negative. Let's not complain. Let's get into the Word of God and let's get ahold of HIS WORDS and let's change the direction that our situation is headed. Let's walk through it differently. **That's what sets us apart.** That's how you live in victory every day, because people in the world do not have this benefit. Most of them do not know the Word, nor how to "stand on" the Word. Many don't even READ the Word. Some of them may not even have a bible, which is a sad thought. People just don't know, and they just don't realize the power of taking God's words and using those words to walk through their situation. They are at the mercy of whatever is before them, whatever comes.

But listen, we're not going to give power to the negative situations in our lives by describing all the rotten details. We're not going to complain. We're going to use our words. We're going to use God's words! God's words will change our situation. That's why we started this devotional with such basic foundational principles such as you need to know that the Word (the Bible) is God's very word, and if He says it, I believe it! I believe whatever is in the Bible! I believe who HE says I am. I believe I have HIS authority. Get some scriptures from the Word that you can pull out, write on index cards, and place them around your house. Keep them in front of you. Speak TO your mountain (using those cards and through what you've memorized). You will see that your words are powerful! You will know how to walk through whatever your situation is because you have The Word of God as your weapon.

You're going to put the scriptures in your mouth and you're going to speak it out because YOUR words have power. It is *scientifically proven* that there is power in the words you speak. And when you speak GOD'S Word, your words can change an atmosphere, a mood. **They change things.** How priceless is it that we have THE Word of God that we can put in our mouth and then His Word fleshes out in our situation because we are speaking His Word into the situation! We are speaking life! Our words will either acquit us—set us free—or condemn us—declare us wrong or bring our doom. Choose your words wisely. They have power.

There is power in your words.

How did today's principle impact you?

_____

_____

_____

Is this something you practice consistently, or is there any area that needs improvement?

_____

_____

_____

How can you take today's principle and apply it to your daily routine?

_____

_____

_____

Prayer enlisting the Lord's help to grow in this discipline

_____

_____

_____

List five things you are grateful for in the last 24 hours

1._____
2._____
3._____
4._____
5._____

List five dreams or goals that you are expecting to happen

1._____
2._____
3._____
4._____
5._____

List your top five "daily affirmations" based on the Word, starting with "I Am....."

1._____
2._____
3._____
4._____
5._____

List five things you are grateful for in the last 24 hours

1.

2.

3.

4.

5.

List five dreams or wishes you want/expect/plan to happen

List your five daily affirmations based on the Word, starting with "I am..."

NOTES

NOTES

Day 29

Dream and Dream BIG

HABAKKUK 2:2, ESV - "Write the vision, make it plain."

Our principle today is to dream—and dream big! Don't just have little dreams. Dream big! How does the principle of dreaming big help us live in victory every day? Well actually, it plays a HUGE role! The God we serve is a BIG God, and He can do BIG things, and He has good plans for us! His Word tells us so! And we, as HIS children, can live our life thriving, not just surviving. I see way too many Christians that are just barely surviving, barely making it, and they're not thriving. At all. God wants us to live in victory every day to the point that we are thriving in life, not merely surviving. In today's devotional, I want to personally share with you something the Lord shared with me about today's principle.

It was the start of a new year. Many people come into a new year full of things that they want to accomplish, resolutions and things that they want to do differently, or just do better. And this was me. At the beginning of this particular year, I thought, "I'm going to do my vision board." I had procrastinated long enough on getting this done. "I'm going to get fresh on my goals and everything for this year. And I'm going to put it where I can see it and dream about it." Habakkuk 2:2 says, *"Write the vision, make it plain."* That's what I did.

My vision board is simply a decorated cork board that has my top eight goals and dreams on it. I finished it, then as I looked over it, I found myself thinking this about several of my dreams, "Oooh, that one's TOO big! It's just too big!" In my humanness, I found myself wondering if or how that dream could ever happen (although I put it right up there on my vision board as if it's going to happen!). Now, I'm not proud to admit that was what my thought process, but that's exactly what I was thinking about a few of them, because they are really big dreams and really big goals! Certainly too big for me to make happen myself! But we are told in scripture to write down the vision and make it plain.

And that's what I did—though it was mixed with a little doubt as to whether those dreams and goals would be attainable. And here's what God said to me in response to my stinking thinking, "Terri, if you can make your dreams happen in your own strength, then you are not dreaming big enough. Dream bigger." Okay then. Yes, I do have some really big dreams on my vision board. And yes, He just spoke to me in direct response to my earlier thoughts. And no, I cannot make these dreams happen in my own strength. I kept thinking about His statement and I just felt like God was reminding me that if I can make my own dreams and goals happen, then would I even need His help? What I knew in that moment was I had to keep dreaming of things that only He can do for me. I had to keep those BIG DREAMS up there on my vision board, because God knows that they are BIG and I could not make them happen in my own power. If I don't dream big then I'm limiting the most powerful force in the universe, God Himself, from stepping in and fulfilling the Ephesians 3:20 *"above all I can ask, think or imagine"* kind of dreams that are on my vision board! God Himself, MY Father!

To continue His reminders to me, I opened up a brand-new devotional book that I have entitled, *Live Your Dreams,* by Terri Savelle Foy. Although I have owned this book for some time, I had not yet read one page. And guess what DAY ONE'S title was? And I quote, "Your Dreams Should Be Impossible." Okay God, I hear you. Listen to a few quotes from this book by Terri Savelle Foy. "I have discovered that God wants your dreams so big and so outside the realm of possibility that naturally speaking there is no way for your dream to happen." "There is no way your dream can occur unless you use your faith." See how faith slipped right in there? When dreaming the impossible—those big, big dreams that you can't make happen on your own—you're going to have to believe that GOD is going to help you bring them to pass! You must have FAITH in God, and you must USE that faith to settle in your mind and your spirit that God can do what seems impossible!

Hebrews 11:6 says, *"Without faith, it is impossible to please God."* In her book, Terri says, "I interpret that scripture to mean that if your dreams are impossible and demand that you have faith in God, then you probably got the right dream." She goes on to say, "Your dreams should stretch you, challenge you and force you to grow." Hebrews 11:1 in the New Living Translation says, *"Faith is the confidence that what we hope for will actually happen. It gives us assurance about things we cannot see."* WOW! God wants us to have dreams and goals that require a giant step of faith, and He wants our total dependency to be on Him in order to see our dreams manifest.

As we close today, I ask you, "If your dreams are possible and YOU can make them happen, WHY do you need GOD to help you?" If that's the case for you, then you're just not dreaming big enough because God has BIG plans for you—plans that only HE can accomplish in your life—and HE wants to bring them to fruition for you and with you! And if by chance you haven't even begun dreaming yet, I challenge you to start! Get some dreams. Get some goals. You need to start dreaming!

Dream and dream BIG.

How did today's principle impact you?

_____

_____

_____

_____

_____

Is this something you practice consistently, or is there any area that needs improvement?

_____

_____

_____

_____

How can you take today's principle and apply it to your daily routine?

_____

_____

_____

_____

Prayer enlisting the Lord's help to grow in this discipline

_____

_____

_____

_____

_____

List five things you are grateful for in the last 24 hours

1._____
2._____
3._____
4._____
5._____

List five dreams or goals that you are expecting to happen

1._____
2._____
3._____
4._____
5._____

List your top five "daily affirmations" based on the Word, starting with "I Am....."

1._____
2._____
3._____
4._____
5._____

NOTES

Day 30

Get a Plan

*JAMES 2:26, GOOD NEWS Translation, - "So then, as the body without the spirit is dead, **also faith without actions is dead.**"*

Yesterday I pointed out how God showed me that I was dreaming too small, and that I needed to dream bigger. Today's principle is going to be the second thing He told me, which was to **get a plan.** This is part two, continuing on from yesterday. "Get a plan." First let me remind you that if you haven't established any goals or dreams for yourself, and you don't have anything you're moving toward, that would be your first step to do. Set some goals and dreams for yourself. You do this by just sitting alone with God, dreaming and talking it over with Him. From yesterday, we saw where Habakkuk 2:2 says to *"Write down your vision. Make it plain."* So that's your first step—find some goals and dreams that you want to move toward. Then write them down. Make them plain. Dream big. Don't let anything be a limit for you. **Dream big.** Yesterday we covered that we should dream big dreams that require big steps of faith—so big that we have to rely on God to see them manifest.

Now let's look at today's principle that says, "get a plan." James 2:26 tells us that *"faith without works or without **action** is dead."* So, I settled into the second thing He told me, get a plan, which makes perfect sense when reading this verse from James. There must be action behind your dreams. Otherwise, your faith is dead and not profitable. Again, that makes perfectly good sense because, honestly, how am I going to move toward the things on my vision board if I don't have a plan of action to take? I mean, for example, being debt free is number one on my list. Being at a certain weight and losing weight is number three on my list. And so, while I would love to walk into my backyard and pull money off of a money tree, and while I know God owns the cattle on a thousand hills and He can do anything He wants at any time, I have to know that He expects me to do my part. My part as a believer would be to tithe, which was one of our principles. I not only tithe, but I sow. And the Bible tells us that you reap what you sow, another one of our principles. Those are two important things for me to do as a plan of action for my finances (goal #1), but I'm already doing those. So, what other things can I do? How else can I set money aside and save? I can choose to limit my spending on excessive coffee runs or going out to eat. I can be a good steward of the things He gives me. That will help me set some money back and save more. Then I can apply it to my debt. If I want to become debt free, I must get serious and put every little bit of extra income I have toward my debt. I can declutter my closet or house decor and sell things on Facebook marketplace or even sell my husband's stuff —haha—you know what I'm saying! Every little bit helps! I just have to have a plan.

And then to lose weight and get healthier, another goal on my vision board, well, I've got to make sure I'm exercising and moving my body. Getting my steps in. Increasing my water intake. Eating cleaner, less sugar, fewer sodas. Getting enough sleep. These are super practical and obvious steps to take to ensure there is a plan in place. And I need to be aware of and intentional about these every day. When I do MY part, God comes and He puts his SUPER on top of my NATURAL and woo-hoo! We'll see those big dreams come to reality.

Now for every one of you that already has a clear picture of your goals and dreams—you have sat with God and you've prayed, you've talked with Him, you've dreamed with Him, and you've written out your goals, you are ready for the next step. (Remember that if you haven't done this already, this is step one.) Then review your dreams/goals regularly. Create a vision board. It doesn't have to be fancy or decorated—just create it and keep it in sight. Then, don't be surprised if God nudges you like He did me and tells you that it's time to step out, get a plan and put action behind your faith. It is then that you will begin to see those big dreams come to pass.

One of my favorite women in the Bible, maybe a very unlikely woman to some, is Rahab. And she actually did just what we're talking about. You see Rahab was a prostitute in the city of Jericho, a Canaanite woman living in Jericho. And she had heard all the stories about the God of Israel—all the victories that He had won in the past—and she believed in Him. Please understand that wasn't what her city and her culture dictated, but she just knew in her heart that the God of Israel, was the real deal. The real God. And if He said He was coming to wipe out Jericho, she knew He was going to do it, and she wanted to be on HIS side. She had a Hebrews 11 kind of faith! She heard of the things that happened with this God and she chose to believe in someone she didn't even know. And boy did it flesh out in a good way for her! She declared her faith in the God of Israel. She believed wholeheartedly (another one of our principles) that He would do to Jericho exactly what He said He would do. So she put **action** behind her faith. And when the spies came to the city of Jericho, she took a big risk, and she helped them by hiding them. She went against culture, against her city. This step was so big that it could have cost her her life. **It could have cost her her life!** She risked everything—not only her life, but the lives of her family.

She could have lost everything, but she didn't. Instead, she gained everything! She gained everything because she took that big, giant step of faith. Although Jericho was destroyed—wiped out—she was saved, and her entire family too! She gained freedom. She gained protection. She gained her life and the lives of her family. And she gained her husband—she ended up marrying one of the spies that she hid! She became his wife and was now a part of his tribe, the children of Israel, worshipping the very God that she so wholeheartedly believed in. Not only was she now one of the children of Israel, but she was in the **direct bloodline of Jesus**! Wow! She gained a place in the bloodline of Jesus. I think that's amazing. (To read more on Rahab's life and story, you will find her in Joshua chapter 2.)

I'm here to tell you today to get some BIG dreams. Exercise some BIG faith. Take a bold step of faith and put action behind your dreams and just see what God will do. You can do this!

Get a plan.

How did today's principle impact you?

_____

_____

_____

_____

_____

Is this something you practice consistently, or is there any area that needs improvement?

_____

_____

_____

_____

How can you take today's principle and apply it to your daily routine?

_____

_____

_____

_____

Prayer enlisting the Lord's help to grow in this discipline

_____

_____

_____

_____

List five things you are grateful for in the last 24 hours

1._____

2._____

3._____

4._____

5._____

List five dreams or goals that you are expecting to happen

1._____

2._____

3._____

4._____

5._____

List your top five "daily affirmations" based on the Word, starting with "I Am....."

1._____

2._____

3._____

4._____

5._____

NOTES

_____
_____
_____
_____
_____
_____
_____
_____
_____
_____
_____
_____
_____
_____
_____

Day 31

We are Blessed to Be a Blessing

GENESIS 12:2, ESV - *"And I will make of you a great nation, and I will bless you and make your name great, so that you will be a blessing."*

Deuteronomy 28:1, ESV - *"And if you faithfully obey the voice of the Lord your God, being careful to do all his commandments that I command you today, the Lord your God will set you high above all the nations of the earth."*

Proverbs 11:25, MSG - *"The one who blesses others is abundantly blessed; those who help others are helped."*

The word "blessing" here means **a liberal giver for God's purpose**. Or we could say that He wants us to be blessed so that we can be liberal givers for His purpose, for the purpose of building His kingdom. When we align with His purpose and His kingdom, and do things HIS way, then He always provides us opportunities so that we can give out to others! We are blessed to be a blessing!

I definitely don't have to ask you if you want to be prosperous, blessed, and succeed in all things. I know you do—just like I do! So, we are going to put all these 31-day principles in place and do our part. God will definitely do His part and put his "super" on our "natural"! Set-backs, failures and disappointments will come, but we carry on—moving forward with Jesus! His way is always better. It's the BEST! **Refuse** to stay bogged down! Get up! Give thanks (have a heart of gratitude)! God's not done with you yet! Set your sights on where you want to go (dream big and get a plan). Make positive affirmations beginning TODAY! Declare that the best, most blessed and prosperous days of your life are just beginning!

Give thanks for where you are, and then simply choose to believe (make it your resolve) that you have a GOOD Heavenly Father who loves you and ALWAYS wants to give you good things! He will bless you so that you will be a blessing! That is His way of doing things.

We cannot give out to the full extent of what God wants us to if we are broken, deflated and defeated, barely surviving. In order for us to maximize being a blessing to others, we must decide daily to do all we can to live according to God's principles. God's desire is for us to be strong and to thrive in every circumstance. IF we do things HIS way, we are ensured to get through every valley and situation that comes our way. With God by our side, leading the way. In closing, I leave you with John 16:33, in the Amplified version, *"I have told you these things, so that in Me you may have [perfect] peace. In the world you have tribulation and distress and suffering, but be courageous [be confident, be undaunted, be filled with joy]; I have overcome the world." [My conquest is accomplished, <u>My victory abiding</u>.]"* Jesus said, ***"...My victory abiding."*** Friends, He has blessed you to be a blessing to those around you. And because of HIS abiding victory, we can do that!

We can be all that He says we can be! HIS will for us is to live each day in victory—thriving not just surviving, whether on the mountaintop or in the valley! I'd like to close this 31-days with a prayer of agreement over each one of you: *Father God, thank you for ALL that you've done for us, in us and through us. I pray for wisdom, direction, blessings and favor for every person here. Help us God to live out Your will, here on earth, as it is in heaven! In Jesus' Name, Amen.*

How did today's principle impact you?

_____

_____

_____

_____

Is this something you practice consistently, or is there any area that needs improvement?

_____

_____

_____

How can you take today's principle and apply it to your daily routine?

_____

_____

_____

_____

Prayer enlisting the Lord's help to grow in this discipline

_____

_____

_____

_____

List five things you are grateful for in the last 24 hours

1._____

2._____

3._____

4._____

5._____

List five dreams or goals that you are expecting to happen

1._____

2._____

3._____

4._____

5._____

List your top five "daily affirmations" based on the Word, starting with
"I Am....."

1._____

2._____

3._____

4._____

5._____

List five things you are grateful for in the last 24 hours:

1.

2.

3.

4.

5.

List five dreams or goals that you are expecting to happen:

1.

2.

3.

I am writing my five daily affirmations based on the 5% on turning with "I am…"

NOTES

_____
_____
_____
_____
_____
_____
_____
_____
_____
_____
_____
_____
_____
_____

About the Author

Terri Sparks

Terri Sparks is a Bible teacher, speaker, and passionate follower of Jesus who loves encouraging others to live out God's Word in their everyday lives. She serves alongside her husband as Senior Pastors in her local church and mentors women in discovering their identity in Christ. Terri enjoys time with family, reading and pool time, and sharing the truth of God's promises through her writing and speaking engagements.